Bandits and Bureaucrats

By

Basha O'Reilly

Author's note: Some names in this book have been changed to protect
the privacy of those concerned.

Cover image: The first ride the author ever took on Count Pompeii.

This book is dedicated to CuChullaine, without whose unending love, help and support this book would never have been written

Our route from Russia to Poland

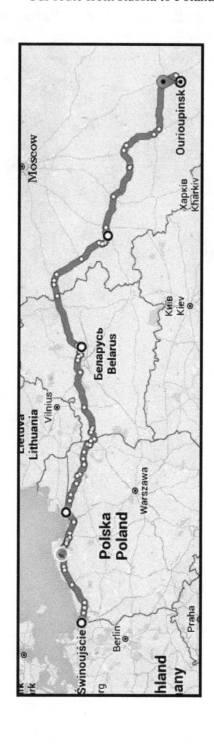

PREFACE

It will be seen from the following pages that, although my 1995 journey was a success, it was not without problems, both foreseen and unforeseen – some of them unforeseeable!

Apart from *Tschiffely's Ride*, I had read nothing about making a long trip on horseback and thought I was unique!

If only I had known that I was following in a long and honourable tradition of passionate equestrian travel, if only I had known what obstacles lay in my path – "if only", two words that rank in my mind with "too late" as being the saddest in the English language.

With the benefit of that wonderful thing, hindsight, I would have done many things differently. At the time I just did the best I could do with the very limited knowledge at my disposal.

It was only when my husband CuChullaine released *The Horse Travel Handbook* in 2016 that our generation of equestrian travellers made a startling collective discovery. We realised that those of us making journeys in the late twentieth century were 'the lost generation'. Because we were too late for the cavalry and too early for the Internet we suffered from a serious lack of equestrian travel wisdom.

I have set out in some detail my problems with the bureaucrats because I know those challenges have not disappeared but, indeed, only got worse.

As it turned out, my trip *was* unique: I am the only person to have ridden out of the former Soviet Union in the entire twentieth century.

Looking back, I understand now what I didn't know at the time. Stalin was behind me, Putin had yet to take power. The Iron Curtain had fallen and all the rules which had been brutally dictated by the Soviet Union had not been replaced – yet.

In this historical bubble of liberty and opportunity I rode across Russia like a shadow. People who had been taught to follow blindly all the rules dictated from distant Moscow were left to make individual decisions on how to react to me.

INTRODUCTION

I don't know why, but I turned to look at some more horses tied to an old cart.

There I saw a scrawny chestnut with white legs and a huge white blaze on his face. His flaxen mane was full of burrs. The bottom of his pale tail had been hacked off with a knife. He was pathetically thin. Physically there was nothing to recommend him. Yet the chestnut looked at me, not in supplication but as an equal – and the expression on his face quite clearly said, "Oh, here you are at last!"

I turned to Vassily. *"Vot etat, pajalusta. Kak yevo zavood?"* (This one, please. What is his name?)

Vassily turned towards me. *"Count Pompeii. No – astarojna! On darogy – y ny loshad dla jenshina!"* ("Count Pompeii. But be careful! He's expensive – and not a horse for a woman!")

I determined to ride him immediately.

Reluctantly, Vassily gave me a leg up. He then jumped onto another horse and shot off across the Russian steppes at a gallop, leaving me to follow as best I could.

Pompeii's head shot up. His small ears turned back and we set off in hot pursuit.

On the horizon the enormous blanched sky blended with the infinite snowy steppes. There were no fences. No hedges. No obstacles at all. I felt as if I had been transported onto the film set of Dr Zhivago.

I crouched down in the saddle and gave Pompeii his head. The wind whistled past my ears, Pompeii's hooves drummed on the frozen ground. My stirrups were too short. I hardly dared breathe the sub-zero air which was burning my lungs. My face, the only uncovered part of me, felt like a block of ice. Tears of cold were blurring my vision. My fingers and toes had lost all feeling.

Pompeii was thoroughly enjoying himself.

So was I.

What, you may ask, was a privileged, middle-aged Englishwoman like me doing galloping across the steppes of Mother Russia with a bunch of Cossacks?

What was it that had prompted me to leave everything I knew and loved and take a huge leap out of my comfort zone – just to find a horse?

Would Pompeii and I survive a journey of 2,500 miles from Russia to my faraway home in England?

If so, would I be able to control a wild Cossack stallion in that sleepy English village?

Turn the page, dear reader, and you will find out!

CHAPTER 1 – HOW IT ALL BEGAN

Sitting at the table in the alcove of Joan's huge kitchen, warmed by the kitchen stove and peopled by half a dozen borzoi dogs, we were drinking wine and chatting about nothing in particular, just enjoying each other's company. Joan's husband had died of cancer about a year earlier, and we had become very close as I had tried to support her through her torment at watching him suffer, then her grief when he finally died.

The borzois lay languidly around us – big enough to put their paws on my shoulders and look down into my face, they were entirely in proportion to the enormous English manor house in which they lived. Long narrow heads, long rangy bodies, long silky fur: they had been bred for centuries to hunt and kill the Russian wolf.

The December rain bucketed down, drenching the beautiful thoroughbred mares in the paddocks outside and dancing on the surface of the lake.

"I've been invited to the Moscow Dog Show again next year. Why don't you come with me this time?" Joan asked casually.

Moscow?

In glamorous, secretive, forbidden Russia?

Boris Yeltsin was in power, the Iron Curtain was disintegrating, Perestroika was in full swing, it was chaos!

How could I refuse?

The recession in Britain in the early 1990s had ensured that my computer training work had almost completely dried up. My husband Andrew was paying the daily bills for the first time in our married life because he was an insolvency practitioner – helping companies and people who had gone bankrupt. My daughter and his sons were grown up.

I was restless.

Excitement and adventure beckoned.

I looked at Joan. Her short dark hair, streaked with silver now, was slightly dishevelled and her green eyes gleamed. Her face was flushed from the wine. We had been friends for a long time, united by our love of horses and dogs. I lit another cigarette, inhaled deeply and blew out the smoke.

"Wonderful – I'd love to go!"

As I was feeding my horses that night, it occurred to me belatedly that I would need to learn Russian!

Thanks to my Swiss mother, I speak passable German, and two years at school in a Belgian convent had given me a good working knowledge of French, so I was not in the habit of needing an interpreter.

I bought a Russian language cassette so I could at least learn the basics.

Then came the icing on the cake. A telephone call from Joan.

"Anna Shubkina, one of the judges at the dog show, says we might be going down to the countryside near Volgograd to do field trials for the Moscow borzois. While we're there, would you like to ride with the Cossacks?"

Ride with the Cossacks? How many English people get a chance to jump in a Cossack saddle and gallop across the steppes?

"Wow – that's fantastic – of *course* I would!"

The Cossacks are a group of Russians who have lived around the great rivers Don, Volga and Dniepre since the fifteenth century. They take their name from the Turkic word "kazak," which means "free man" or "adventurer." The poet Pushkin defined them as: "Always on horse-back, always ready to fight, always on the alert." For five hundred years they have been a byword for horsemanship.

Although they are justly famous for their great courage and free spirit, they have never excluded outsiders. If they considered someone a worthy warrior, they would invite him to join their band. Generations of Tsars had relied on free Cossacks to defend and expand Russia's frontiers for four centuries.

Tragically, when the 1917 Bolshevik revolution exploded, the Cossacks' reputation nearly resulted in their annihilation. Stalin had most of them slaughtered or sent to gulags in Siberia. Courage and independence were hardly qualities to be applauded or encouraged by the Communists!

Fierce free spirits can be driven underground but they are not so easily destroyed. Now that communism was in tatters the Cossacks were slowly re-emerging.

Imagine being allowed to ride with them!

I am a horsewoman to my fingertips, so I felt reasonably confident that I would not disgrace myself. From the age of three I have been infatuated with horses, spending all the school holidays dashing about, usually bareback, on a succession of ponies. Unlike most girls, however,

I had not grown out of this obsession when I discovered boys. I had graduated instead from childhood Pony Club events, through hunting, to the study of dressage and three-day-eventing.

My beloved old grey Arab mare, Aysha, lived in the stables facing my kitchen, as did a big bay thoroughbred, Isabel, who belonged to my daughter Katie. I rode them both at every opportunity, hacking for hours round the beautiful Wessex countryside. I had reached the age of 46 and could no longer see the point of going round in circles in a ring. Dressage bored me. Jumping artificial obstacles seemed contrived. Moreover, entering any competition involved loading the horses in a trailer, and for some reason I have always felt that putting horses – themselves a form of transport – into a lorry was absurd.

In the months following Joan's invitation I kept myself busy, tending my garden, riding my horses, and learning Russian.

Meanwhile, I slowly began to acknowledge a growing knot of personal dissatisfaction in my heart. My marriage was a shambles – I knew it, Andrew must have known it, but we never discussed it. Like hundreds of thousands of couples, we just hung onto the status quo. Andrew claimed to love me, but I had finally admitted to myself that he loved my money-earning ability more than my expertise in the kitchen, drawing room or bedroom. I faced the stark reality that my husband was a lazy spendthrift, incredibly quick-tempered and obsessed with prestige and material things.

When I followed Joan into the first-class aircraft cabin that autumn, I had no premonition that this flight to Moscow was to be the start of a much longer, more difficult and exhilarating journey – a voyage into the emotional and physical unknown.

CHAPTER 2 – A JOURNEY TO MOSCOW

We walked out of the aircraft into the cold embrace of Moscow's Sheremetyavo airport. The arrivals lounge had been built at a time when only the Soviet elite were permitted to fly. Now it was struggling to accommodate half a dozen jumbo jet-loads of passengers: two thousand people jammed into a space designed for a maximum of five hundred. The result was typical Russian chaos: long queues, short tempers and a scarcity of *chelliyeshki* (luggage trolleys). With no concept of "service" or, for that matter, of the importance of the individual, the faces of the immigration officials glaring at Joan and me were as surly as they were pasty.

As soon as we had extricated ourselves from the crowds and the bureaucrats and emerged from the tiny airport building, a short, stocky woman launched herself at us, crying, "Joan! Joan!"

"How nice to see you again," Joan said smiling. "Barbara, this is Anna Shubkina – Anna, this is my friend Barbara."

"Pleased to meet you," said Anna, and shook my hand briskly.

Anna Shubkina, a biologist at the Moscow Academy of Sciences, and an expert in Borzoi dogs, was our interpreter and guide. With a Beatles mop of very dark red hair, close-set brown eyes and a hawk nose, she smoked More menthol cigarettes incessantly, and exuded energy. I was to discover that energy is unusual in Russian people.

"Come. I have a flat for you – let us go to the car."

We wound our way through the crowds on the pavement in the cold October air to a tiny, tinny brown Lada which already had a large grizzled old borzoi in it, so I squeezed in the back with him. The smell of dog was overpowering.

We approached the capital at breakneck speed, human and canine passengers thrown about like rag dolls as Anna failed, over and over again, to see the potholes in time. A broken spring was digging into my leg. I felt sick.

In my imagination Russia was completely covered with pine forests, but the trees in the flat landscape were mainly birch trees, now turning soft shades of tangerine, coral and gold. Hundreds of massive rectangular concrete apartment blocks reared up all around us. The roads were wide, crowded with rusty vehicles, and in shocking disrepair. We saw nothing which remotely resembled the breathtaking, improbable beauty of St Basil's Cathedral in Red Square. I grew to love Moscow, but at that time it was – how can I say this diplomatically? – one of the ugliest and least-cared-for cities I had ever known.

Eventually the car drew up outside one of the hideous buildings, and we all clambered out. I tried to brush off some of the dog hairs which clung tenaciously to my clothes, but without noticeable success. The lift was out of order, so we hauled our luggage up two flights of stairs.

"This is the apartment of Sasha," announced Anna, opening the door to one of the flats.

Joan and I looked around us with dismay. There was nothing remotely welcoming about that flat – tatty old furniture had been placed randomly around the rooms, the curtains were old, dirty and shabby, and a stale, strange smell hung in the air. Everything was painted or upholstered in varying shades of brown.

"I will fetch you tomorrow," Anna called over her shoulder, and left.

Well, at least the place was warm. I dumped our bags in the bedroom while Joan opened the bottle of vodka she had bought in the duty-free shop at Heathrow Airport, five hours and a lifetime ago.

"Welcome to Moscow!" Joan said as she poured a generous measure into each of the two cracked glasses I'd found.

The following day Joan and I sat around waiting for Anna. By lunchtime we were worried - and hungry. Where was she? Joan had her telephone number but there was no reply when we dialled it. When our telephone rang, I looked at it in dismay. Should I answer it? It might be Anna. It might not be Anna – what would I say then? I picked the receiver up nervously.

"*Da?*" (Yes?)

"*Dobraya outra*" said a male voice. "*Sasha, pajalusta?*" ("Good morning. Is Sasha there please?")

"*Nyet,*" I replied, "*Izvineetya, Sasha nyet.*" ("Sorry, no Sasha.") It was the best I could do. I hung up, as disappointed as the caller must have been.

I went into the kitchen to look for something to eat. I opened a cupboard. The handle was sticky. Behind the door were a few tins with pictures of meat on the labels, an ancient packet of rice, some mouse-droppings and half a dozen cockroaches. I shut the door hastily. I looked cautiously in the refrigerator – it contained only some mouldy, rock-hard cheese and a couple of decaying tomatoes.

"Sorry, Joan" I apologised as I walked back into the sitting room. "There's not a scrap to eat here!"

Five minute later the front door opened and Anna bustled in without any apology or explanation for the delay.

"Tomorrow we go down to the village of Alexikovo to see the borzoi dogs" she told us. "Now, let's visit my father where we can eat."

It was 3 p.m. Another bone-breaking, heart-stopping drive in her little car brought us to a concrete block, one of a dozen identical buildings set among a pine forest in Konkovo, a suburb on the outskirts of Moscow. The lift was out of order, so we climbed to the third floor. I was to discover that Moscow lifts seldom worked – pity the mother who had to lug her shopping up to the twelfth floor, possibly carrying a small child!

Joan and I stood on the landing, getting our breath back, while Anna opened an insubstantial door.

"This is my father, Vladimir Shubkin" Anna announced once we had crowded into the small flat. "He speaks English." I shook his outstretched hand and smiled into his welcoming blue eyes. He was my height (5'6"), with close-cropped white hair, a stocky body, and a deeply wrinkled face. He must have been at least seventy-five because I soon discovered that he was a veteran of the bloody conflict at Stalingrad (which had now been given back its original name, Volgograd).

The four of us squashed ourselves around the tiny table, tucking into the boiled chicken which Anna had cooked, and discussed the journey to Alexikovo.

"My friend Julia is also coming, with her two dogs and her son. The train will leave at 8 p.m. and arrives at about 6 o'clock the following morning."

"How far is it to Alexikovo?" I asked as I handed the salt cellar to Joan, thinking that a ten-hour train journey surely ought to transport us half-way across Russia.

"Six hundred kilometres."

That was about 450 miles, so we would be averaging 45 m.p.h.

"Russian trains are hardly in competition with the French TGV (*Trains de Grande Vitesse*, which travel at speeds up to 200 m.p.h.)" I thought.

Vladimir had put a bottle of Georgian wine called "Kinsmarooli" on the table and topped up our glasses while I interrogated Anna about

Russian names. I remembered being totally confused while reading "War and Peace" in my teens.

"It's very simple," she assured me. "We each have a first name (*Imir*), a patronymic name (*Ochestva*) taken from our father's first name, and a family name (*Familie*). Therefore my full name is Anna Vladimir-nova Shubkina."

"What if you had been a boy?"

"Then I would have been Nikolai (for example) Vladimiravitch Shubkin."

I could not agree that it was very simple, but at last I understood the logic. And afterwards, when I realised how few Christian names there are in Russia, I also understood the necessity.

Another frightening car journey brought us back to Sasha's flat. Anna let us in, and abruptly left us. "See you tomorrow. I have the train tickets."

There was still no sign of Sasha.

The Russian word for "railway station" is "*Vagzall*." Tsar Nikolai, on a visit to England in the nineteenth century, had seen the London station, Vauxhall, and asked what it was called. He had meant, of course, to ask what the English word for "station" was.

As soon as the Tsar returned home he called for a pen and a ruler and he drew a line between Moscow and St. Petersburg. It wasn't quite a straight line, as the finger holding the ruler down had projected very slightly over the edge. "Build me a railway to join Russia's two most beautiful cities," he ordered. His instructions were slavishly obeyed – of course – and the resulting railway line has a little curve in it at the point where His Highness's finger had interrupted the pen.

The *Vagzall* Anna brought us to the following afternoon was vast, crowded and the first beautiful building we had seen. Elegant columns arched serenely high above our heads. On the ground, by contrast, Russians bustled about busily. Warmly wrapped against the autumn chill, the Slavs' dreary brown and faded grey clothing was in sharp contrast to that of the Central Asians who mingled with them. These colourful people, who came from Kazakhstan, Uzbekistan and Turkmenistan, dressed in scarlet and amber, vivid blues and brilliant greens.

The Russians have a very sensible system of numbering not only the trains, but also the carriages. This makes life very simple even for foreigners. The three of us walked down the platform with our luggage in search of our carriage.

"Here it is!" exclaimed Anna, and climbed up the steps. Following her example, we threaded our way along the corridor until Anna found our compartment, a four-berth sleeper. A dark-haired, bespectacled, slim young woman sitting on one of the bunks was introduced to us as Julia. Her ten-year-old son Nikolai and two borzoi dogs were also there. I stared around the tiny, overheated cabin in disbelief: there were four adults, two enormous dogs and the child – where would we all sleep? There was not even room for us all to stand up in the small space between the bunks.

I thought back to previous overnight train journeys from Zürich to Paris, from London to Aberdeen, and a trip across Canada, recalling the luxury of a sleeping compartment to myself. But this was Russia, so that night I shared one of the bottom bunks with a dog – a perfectly nice dog, granted, but large, hairy, restless and smelly nonetheless.

The train pulled out, only fifteen minutes late. I had been much amused, listening to my Russian language cassettes, to learn that the Russian phrase for "Is the train on time?" actually translates literally as, "Is the train not late?" We trundled slowly through the countryside, stopping frequently for no apparent reason.

I woke up from a fitful slumber at 5 a.m., but everyone else was still asleep. The train was still proceeding at its unhurried pace, so I wondered how much later than the specified time we would arrive at our destination. I got dressed and set off down the corridor to find the *dijournaya* (attendant).

"*Xatitye chai?*" she offered. ("Would you like some tea?")

"*Da, pajalusta*" I said gratefully. I was shivering, and could see that the boiler had burned up its allocation of coal and gone out.

She handed me a glass of steaming, sweet, black tea – no charge. She hadn't asked how I liked it, because sweet and black is how all Russians drink both tea and coffee.

Telling the time in Russian is so complicated that I didn't dare ask what time we were due in to Alexikovo. I knew I probably wouldn't have understood the answer, even if I had not been exhausted. "Five past six," for example, translates as "Five minutes of the seventh hour."

So, sipping the hot tea, I walked slowly back down the corridor, past our cabin, to the opposite end of the carriage. This was the only place I could smoke – it was a pity that it was right outside the lavatory which, after many long hours of travel, reeked of urine.

I had only just got back to our compartment when the train stopped. We had arrived! The five of us piled out of the train, the dogs barking excitedly and getting tangled up in their leads. Russian curses filled the cold air. It was 7.15 a.m. and the sun was just preparing to emerge. Alongside a small brick building was a black Lada, and leaning against this car was a short man in his late twenties, sporting a sandy moustache and a fur hat.

"*Privyet*, Nikolai," Anna cried and offered her cheek to be kissed. She had already warned us that none of the Cossacks spoke English, so as we shook hands I said, "*Zdrastvoytye*" – "Hello."

Nikolai looked at Joan and me with open curiosity, greeted me in return, and turned to open the car doors. Somehow six people and two dogs all managed to squeeze inside a car built for four midgets. Nikolai got behind the wheel and we set off. Joan and I sat in silence as the Russians chatted among themselves, speaking far too quickly for me to understand even the gist of what they were saying. I contented myself with staring at the steppes around us. I had expected a vast, flat, treeless landscape, covered in long grass, but the ground undulated to the horizon and the grass was short. Small woods, hardly more than copses, were dotted liberally around, and on each side of the arrow-straight road was a *passadka* – a row of tall trees.

After a couple of miles along the tarmac road, we turned onto a muddy track. We bumped along uncomfortably for several more miles before Nikolai turned onto an even smaller cart track which led us to a cluster of primitive small houses. He pulled up outside one of these and we all got out into a dirty farmyard. A handsome borzoi was tethered to a tree, while four more were leaping hysterically and barking in a small run.

"Come in! Come in!" ordered Anna as she made her way towards the house. We stumbled up the steps to a small porch. "Take your boots off and put on some of these shoes." We obeyed, and followed Anna through a door into a warm kitchen. Inside, a couple got up from a rickety table, smiling rather nervously.

"Please meet Piotr and Nadyezhda," Anna said, and turned to our hosts. "*Eta Joan y Barbara*." Nods and smiles followed this simple introduction, and we were urged to sit down and have some chai.

Piotr was a skinny man with thinning dark hair, brown eyes and beige teeth, dressed in shabby trousers and an ancient blue shirt. I thought he was about sixty until I saw the numbers tattooed on his knuckles – 1947. He was the same age as I was. His wife Nadyezhda was fat and cheerful. Her smile revealed a few gold teeth. Her curly brown hair reached her shoulders, and she wore a green nylon dress with floral sprigs. Her work-worn hands were busy pouring chai, adding sugar, stirring.

After my early-morning chai on the train I needed the loo. Piotr's house was little more than a shack, so there was not only no bathroom, there was no running water – it all had to be fetched from the village well. To go to the loo I was directed to a small, stinking shed round the back of the house. Inside I discovered two things: a hole in the ground and torn-up squares of old newspaper which were neatly stacked by the door for use as lavatory paper. As I squatted there in the dark, I wondered how either of my grandmothers – the wealthy, aristocratic English one or the elegant, artistic Swiss one – would have viewed the situation.

Back in the warmth of the kitchen, I stared curiously around me, surprised to see kitsch posters of impossibly cuddly kittens on the walls. The linoleum on the floor needed replacing. The crockery was chipped. A stale, but not unpleasant, odour clung to the walls and flaky ceiling.

Nadyezhda carried a steaming pot to the table – boiled meat and potatoes – and we all tucked in. The food was edible, and no doubt nourishing, but the meat was tough and tasteless. Anna opened the bottle of vodka we had brought. I was surprised to see that Piotr did not have any – a Russian refusing vodka? Impossible! Anna explained in her rather broken English.

"A long time ago, during some local elections, Piotr drinks too much vodka and rides his horse into an official building. For this bad behaviour and insult to the Communist Party, they send him to Siberia for ten years! Since then he never drinks."

I looked again at his tired lined face. Small wonder he had aged so badly.

After we had eaten and drunk our fill, it was time to go to the "camp" where the Muscovites had parked themselves and their dogs. We all jumped back in the car and drove off, waving goodbye to Piotr and Nadyezhda.

A quarter of an uncomfortable hour later the Lada jolted into a forest and drew up outside a long, low wooden building. We extricated our-

selves stiffly from the car. Borzois by the dozen were boiling and seeth-
ing around. Several men and women came out of the building to greet
us.

The undisputed chief of the gang was Tariq, a Georgian. He was
larger than life in every sense. Six foot four inches in height, he was
almost as big around, with arms as thick as my thighs. His shoulder-
length white hair and vigorous beard gave him the appearance of a pagan
god – Neptune!

"*Ochin pryatna*" ("Pleased to meet you"). His rich, dark-brown
voice boomed as he enfolded my small hand in his huge, grimy paw.
"*Ochin pryatna*," I responded feebly.

This simple exchange of civilities convinced Tariq that I was a fluent
Russian-speaker, and for the rest of our stay he insisted on jabbering at
me at full speed, not one whit put out by the fact that my unvarying
response to anything much more complex than "hello" was "*Ya nye
panimayo*" ("I don't understand").

We all went into the building for supper – it was laid out like an army
barracks, with one room containing a vast refectory table, beyond which
two doors led to the male and female dormitories and another into the
kitchen. More stewed meat was accompanied (of course) by vodka, and
the toasts became more and more garbled as the level in the bottles sank
rapidly. I discovered it was *de rigeur* to drink as the Russians do – gulp
the lot at once. It was useless to protest that in England we sip vodka
with tonic, ice, and lemon. "*Nyet!*" bellowed Tariq, obviously genuinely
offended. "*Pa-Russki!*" (in the Russian manner). "*Tagda choot-choot*,"
("In that case, just a little") I said.

Anna, Julia and little Nikolai were all due to stay at this borzoi camp,
but Joan and I had been booked into a hotel in nearby Alexikovo. Anna
had confidently described it as "a country hotel." After dinner, Nikolai
drove us back to town and stopped the car outside a two-storey, off-white
dilapidated building. We unfolded ourselves from the car, retrieved our
bags from the boot, and Anna led us through a wide door into a dim
lobby.

The clerk behind the counter was as unwelcoming as he was un-
kempt, not bothering to conceal the contempt in his voice. He had
clearly not attended the Swiss school of hotel management.

"*Passporty!*," he commanded.

We meekly handed over our passports for him to check.

After Anna left, Joan and I climbed the rickety staircase to the first floor, gagging at the stench as we passed the one and only lavatory. I opened the door to our room. Joan gasped. Two ancient iron beds squatted on the sloping floor, with grubby blankets roughly thrown over them. The window was thick with cobwebs, and the smell of decades of unwashed bodies was impossible to ignore.

"Oh dear," I sighed philosophically, "which bed do you want?"

"I don't want either of them!" Joan wailed. Brought up in a cocoon of wealth and privilege, my friend was not accustomed to such primitive conditions. Neither was I, but somehow the promise of riding with the Cossacks made these minor inconveniences completely irrelevant.

"Well, we're stuck here now" I reasoned. "Perhaps we can ask for another room tomorrow." Silly of me – only a cock-eyed western optimist would have believed a different room would be an improvement on our sorry quarters.

In a fury, Joan threw her suitcase on one of the beds and pulled off her Hermes scarf. It must have cost her about £200, and I daresay she could have bought the entire hotel for a similar sum.

"But Anna said we'd be staying in a country hotel!" she muttered. "This is not what I imagined."

"I'm tired," I said, hoping to prevent a major sulk on Joan's part. I opened my suitcase and dug out my sponge-bag. "I'm going down to clean my teeth."

The corridor at the foot of the stairs still smelt revolting.

I opened the door to the lavatory cautiously. There was one basin – the only one in the hotel – and one loo. The latter was overflowing, and the floor was an inch deep in water and… I ran back upstairs.

"First time in my life I've had to put wellington boots on before cleaning my teeth" I said to Joan, trying to make light of it. She had dug the vodka bottle out of her suitcase again.

We hardly slept that night. The mattresses were hard and lumpy, with springs sticking out in just enough places to make it impossible to avoid them.

It was probably my imagination, but I felt a sudden urge to scratch.

CHAPTER 3 - HUNTING WITH THE COSSACKS

Joan and I left our respective beds at 6 a.m. with no reluctance at all. Before leaving England I had packed my breeches and knee-high leather hunting boots, and while I struggled into them Joan stood in front of the cracked looking glass, winding her hair round a pair of curling tongs. I then watched incredulously as she carefully applied her make-up. Where did she think we were going? Who did she think we were going to meet? This was not Ascot or a similar society event in England. I shrugged and made some coffee – we had brought our own with us.

We didn't have long to wait before Nikolai, who had obviously been designated as our chauffeur, picked us up and drove us back to the Borzoi camp. We travelled in silence, as my vocabulary was exhausted. There in the dining room we found a throng of Muscovites, Cossacks and dogs. The warm smell of stew drifted out of the big pan on the table. Chai was poured. Vodka bottles were opened. *"Choot-choot"* I cried ineffectually. I'll drink as much as the next guy, but not at 7 a.m.

A huge Russian army truck known as a "66" appeared after breakfast and all sixteen of us, along with innumerable borzois, climbed in the back. The field trials were about to begin at last! After half an hour of lumbering along rutted tracks, the "66" lurched to a stop beside a small wood and we jumped to the ground. I could hardly contain my excitement. Any minute now I'd be settling into the saddle!

A dozen Cossacks – including Nikolai and Piotr – were sitting on their horses under the trees at the appointed rendezvous to inspect us. They looked remarkably alike: dressed in shabby old jackets and trousers, most of them had a moustache. All were wearing fur hats. These gave them a wildly glamorous appearance quite at odds with their cheap clothes. Their horses were small, stocky and seemed docile enough. Black, chestnut, grey, brown – all the usual colours were present. The riders sat comfortably in the saddles and stared at us with open curiosity.

I studied the tack. Some of the bridles were handsomely decorated with silver studs. The rusty iron snaffle bits hung very low in the horses' mouths but, in contrast, the throat lashes were all done up tightly. The reins were joined much closer to the bit than English ones are, leaving five feet of leather trailing for use as a whip.

"You can't ride now" said Anna, anticipating my question.

"Why not?"

"You have to wait," was her only explanation.

The field trials started. Joan and I joined a long line of walkers with dogs, who made their way across the ground, like beaters at an English shoot, while the horsemen followed closely behind. The lines of *passadki* (trees) showed the position of the road, a mile away. It was bitterly cold. The leaden sky hinted at snow to come.

A cry rang out! "*Zayeetsa!*" (A hare!) The nearest borzois were unleashed. Two or three of the riders joined the chase. The hounds hunted with silent menace and astounding speed. I stared after them, my heart pounding. The only sound was the drumming of the galloping hooves on the hard ground. No luck this time: the borzois lost the hare and returned to the nearest horse, as they were trained to do, before accompanying it back to the line of walkers.

The line started again. And again. And again.

It was time for lunch. Bread, cheese, *kalbasi* (a type of salami), vodka.

"Can I ride now?"

"No, not yet."

"Why not?"

"The Cossacks say the horses are not tired enough."

By 4 p.m. I was bitterly disappointed, convinced that for one reason or another, one excuse or another, I was not going to get on a horse that day.

"Barbara! Come over here! You can ride this horse now!"

I could scarcely believe my ears.

One of the Cossacks, Ura Kabil, rushed to help me into the saddle of Nikolai's very pretty chestnut gelding, intriguingly named Parabola. I settled myself in the saddle, patted my mount and picked up the reins.

The line was re-formed and the trials continued.

Parabola and I walked a few yards behind the pedestrians. He was a comfortable ride, and obedient, although he kept wanting to stop and graze. "Oh no," I told him, "not while I'm in the saddle and not while we're working." Having established that I was the boss, and that Parabola did not seem inclined either to rear or to buck, I relaxed and enjoyed being back on a horse.

To my surprise, Anna had also got on a horse. With huge difficulty, shouting "*Trrrr!*" ("whoa!") at it, she had managed to haul herself into the saddle, where she sat proudly in her bright pink track-suit. Frankly, she looked like a garish sack of potatoes, and I hoped she would be able to stay on board for what was left of the day.

There were no more hares found that night. Snowflakes were starting to float out of the sky. It was growing dark, time to call it a day.

A little disappointed by the lack of excitement, I was on the point of dismounting when Anna called out to me.

"Would you like to ride back to Piotr's house?" she asked.

"Oh yes, I'd love to – if the Cossacks don't mind."

Nikolai had swung onto Piotr's big black mare, so we set off together at a spanking trot. It was getting really cold, so I hunted in my pocket for a handkerchief. I had already discovered that the metal hoop on the pommel of my saddle was extremely useful: I could loop the reins over it and let go of them completely while I blew my nose or lit a cigarette.

My Cossack companion was smiling at my nonchalance. He seemed impressed that so far I had not fallen off. We were trotting at breakneck speed across the darkening steppes. I hoped my pretty little horse was sure-footed. On and on we hurtled. Only later did I understand that I was being tested. Nikolai was waiting for me to cry out that I was tired, that I wanted to stop, that I was frightened. But of course I did no such thing – I was perfectly at home in that saddle! Gradually Nikolai's expression changed from polite contempt to grudging respect.

Twenty minutes and four non-stop miles later we were turning in at Piotr's gate. I was aghast – in England we would never dream of bringing in sweating, steaming steeds as Nikolai and I did that evening. We would have brought our horses back to a walk for the last mile or so to let them cool off.

I jumped off, and started trying to undo the girth.

"*Nyet!*" Nikolai grabbed my arm. "*Ni nada.*" (It's not necessary.) Instead, he merely tied the chestnut up in the yard next to the black horse, both animals soaking wet, girths still tight, and walked off. I stood there feeling hideously guilty. Then I reminded myself that this was Russia. Things were done differently here. If a horse wasn't tough enough to stand this sort of treatment, then he was in the wrong place. I patted my mount, trying pathetically to make it up to him, and walked away reluctantly.

Just as we arrived, Anna and Joan drove up in the "66" with Tariq. We all crowded into the warm little house, laughing and talking. Moments later the door flew open and Ura came in, closely followed by

Lev, another of the Cossacks. Ura's black hair and moustache were set off by brilliant blue eyes while Lev's hair was very blond. They were in their early thirties. They removed their hats, apparently unaware that they thus instantly transformed themselves from mysterious, exciting Cossacks into ordinary, dull men.

More vodka bottles were produced, together with the obligatory *"agourtsi"* – pickled cucumbers. No Russian will ever drink on an empty stomach – the eating of gherkins, preserved tomatoes, or bread was an essential part of the serious business of drinking a toast. Tariq slapped me on the shoulder, laughed and said something. I looked at Anna questioningly.

"Tariq says the Cossacks all think you ride very well!" she said, sounding slightly surprised. She lit a cigarette and smiled at me, showing her stained, uneven teeth.

"Thank you." What could I say? Did life have any more to offer than this: compliments on my riding ability from the *Cossacks* of all people? And yet, I had hardly done anything! Then I understood: if the only woman they had ever seen in the saddle was Anna, well then yes, by comparison I did ride extremely well.

What I didn't know at the time, and what the Cossacks had forgotten, was that in the past Cossack women had ridden, and ridden well. In the early twentieth century, the courageous Russian Alexandra Kudasheva rode through China, Manchuria, Siberia and Europe, then went on to lead 600 Cossacks into battle during the First World War. Yet in 1928 Stalin passed a law making it illegal for private individuals to own a horse, and all memory of women on horseback was forgotten.

For the next three days I was allowed to ride all day, every day, jumping onto whichever animal was made available for me. When a hare was put up near me, I went galloping after the borzois, the thrill of the chase pounding through my veins and bringing back memories of my fox-hunting days in faraway England.

Initially, one of the Cossacks always came with me, in case I was thrown off and had to be scraped off the hard ground, but gradually they came to accept that I was as at home in the saddle as they were.

Towards the end of the last day the borzois did catch their prey. Three of them working together trapped the poor hare and he was dead in an instant. I was right behind them – the only horseman for half a mile.

"Poor thing," I thought, as I galloped up to the bloody scrum. "Oh hell, what do I do now?"

Fortunately Ura had seen my predicament and galloped to my side, shouting at me as he leapt off his horse. He ran over to beat the dogs off the corpse, tied some string to the bloody mess and hung it onto my saddle. As we rode back to join the others, everyone applauded, as though I had achieved some great victory.

"She is one of us now," Ura shouted, and the Cossacks all cheered.

Joan looked enviously at me. I didn't know whether to laugh, look smug, or burst into tears. Being British, of course, I did none of those things: I just grinned stupidly.

That evening as we sat round the table after our farewell supper I was presented with gifts.

"Here is a Cossack bridle for you," said Anna. "They want you to have it because they think you ride so well."

"Please thank these men for their generosity, and tell them how honoured I am to be riding with them."

"And here is a Cossack whip," Anna continued. "I am to tell you that this is what they use to keep their wives in order."

I looked at the smirking men.

"Please thank them again: now I shall have a very obedient husband."

There was a long silence after this was translated, with a giggle, by Anna.

Then the Cossacks roared their approval. *"Da! Da! Byedna Angli-chanin!"* ("Poor Englishman!")

I didn't dare tell the Cossacks what was in my heart – not then. Earlier that day an idea had pushed itself, fully-fledged and totally unexpectedly into my brain. "These horses are so tough, mentally as well as physically, wouldn't it be wonderful to buy some and ride them all the way back to England?"

As far as I knew, nobody had ever made such a trip! I know now that Cossack officer Mikhail Asseev had ridden 2,200 miles from Kiev to Paris in 1889. In the same year, another Cossack, Dmitri Peshkov had set out from the far east of Siberia and ridden 5,500 miles to St. Petersburg.

Much more recently, Jean-Louis Gouraud had ridden 2,500 miles from Paris to Moscow in 1990.

But I had never heard of any of these men, or indeed any person who had undertaken a Long Ride, although I had of course read about Aimé Tschiffely's astonishing ride on two Criollos from Buenos Aires to Washington, D.C.

For all these reasons the logical brain of a spoilt European had kicked in. How could I possibly even contemplate such a mad journey? Where would I stay en route? It would be impossible to organise such a trip, which would probably turn out to be extremely dangerous and uncomfortable. My civilised, privileged, sophisticated side rejected the idea as absurd, but some strange, new, wild part of me refused to let it die.

CHAPTER 4 – CHOOSING THE HORSES

Back in England, I picked up the threads of my old routine.

From the cosy comfort of a small Wessex village, my dream of riding 2500 miles across five countries seemed an irrational fantasy, destined to be stillborn. I had never been on an expedition and had no experience of camping. How could I possibly make this trip?

I mentioned my mad idea, casually, to Andrew – who laughed. Well, I really cannot blame him for being sceptical!

Six months after I returned home, God, clearly impatient with my pathetic inactivity, decided to take a hand and show me the way.

"This isn't my cup of tea, Mummy, but it sounds like just the thing for you," my daughter Katie said, handing me a letter. Colonel John Blashford-Snell, the famous British explorer, was looking for horsemen to go on a month-long expedition in the High Altai mountains of Mongolia.

Why did she say that? Although I was 46 years old, I had never even spent a night in a tent. My privileged parents had always defined "living rough" as being obliged to stay in anything less than a five-star hotel.

The Mongolian expedition would be an expensive trip, but Andrew, obviously sensing we were drifting apart, insisted that I should go.

So I borrowed a rucksack, stuffed it with gear, and headed for Mongolia's capital, Ulaan Baator, with Colonel Blashford-Snell's expedition team.

I acquired a good deal of knowledge while living with the nomadic Mongolian herdsmen.

1. I realised I could get by with very few clothes and no cosmetics.
2. I acquired the knack of packing intelligently and keeping my gear dry.
3. I found out I could live in a tent.
4. I could adapt to a different culture quickly and effortlessly.
5. I found out that the world is not full of bandits, whatever the faint-hearted may tell you.

I enjoyed that month-long expedition enormously. Despite revolting food and incredibly harsh conditions, I was happier than I had been for years.

My husband Andrew met me at Heathrow airport on my return.

"Oh, Barbara, I've missed you – I'm so glad you're home!" he muttered as he hugged me. But I had only one thing on my mind.

"Hello, Andrew. I've discovered how I can ride those horses back from Russia!"

He stared down at me from his height of 6'4". His grey eyes studied me from behind his thick-rimmed spectacles, and he ran his hand despairingly through his short, greying hair.

We got back to our lovely house, set peacefully beside a stream and looking over serene parkland, to the usual hysterical reaction from my five dogs. They were barking, leaping, yelping, and falling over each other in their eagerness to bid me welcome. Although it is true that I had been gone for more than a month, I received a similar reception every time I returned from a one-hour shopping trip. They say animals have no sense of time – certainly my dogs didn't!

When I had finally fought my way past the dogs and into the house, and before I even unpacked, I sent a fax to Anna Shubkina in Moscow.

"I would like to buy some horses from the Cossacks and ride them back to England. I shall fly to Russia at the end of November to choose the animals. Can you please help me organise this?"

The children came home for the weekend to hear about my Mongolian adventures. Instead, over dinner I told them about my plan to buy some Russian horses and ride them home. Andrew's two sons shook their heads in disbelief at my crazy scheme, yet Andrew was surprisingly enthusiastic. It was only later that I understood he foresaw fame and fortune for his wife. Or did he hope that if he let me go, our marriage would miraculously be saved? If so, he cannot have faced the fact that it was his own behaviour which had made me so desperately unhappy.

Katie, however, merely raised her eyebrows and laughed. She knew me too well to be surprised. After dinner, when the men had left the dining room to go and watch television, Katie and I stayed at the table, smoking and finishing the wine. My first marriage had broken up when Katie was only six months old, so we had always been very close.

"Would you like to come with me to choose the horses?" I asked her.

"What? To *Russia*? Oh yes, I'd love to!" She was 24, unattached, and a dyed-in-the-wool horsewoman, so the idea was very attractive to her.

So it was that my daughter and I flew to Moscow, met Anna, and took the same sluggish train down to Volgograd *oblast* (county). This time

Katie and I were invited to stay with Piotr and Nadyezhda in their home, so we were spared the horrors of the "country hotel" which Joan and I had endured on our previous visit.

Nevertheless, Katie was miserable. Winter had taken a firm grip down on the steppes. The food was either tasteless or downright disgusting. Katie didn't like vodka. She was sickened by the outside privy. She caught a cold. She felt wretched.

I loved it.

I had barely drunk my first cup of *chai* when Piotr hustled us outside to show us a really beautiful iron-grey mare called "Rada" (which means "pleased").

"Do you like her?" asked Anna. "She is for sale."

I trotted her around the village.

When I got back, I told Anna, "I do like her, although she seems very flighty. I'll think about it."

"Flighty?" Anna obviously did not know the word.

"Yes – it means lively and not very obedient!"

"Tomorrow we go see some more, then you decide. Now we have dinner."

The following morning Anna borrowed Piotr's Lada and drove Katie and me to a nearby stud to inspect some horses. Although I had of course bought horses before, I was out of my element here in deepest Russia.

The three of us scrambled out of the car into a biting, Siberian wind, and slithered across the broken, icy ground towards an enormous barn. By the door Anna introduced us to Vassily Vadianov, the farm manager. He was a Cossack and proud of it. Dark-haired, burly, red-faced and smiling, he shook my hand shyly.

On our right sixty horses swirled in a vast corral, arguing over mounds of hay, snorting, steaming and stomping in the bitter cold. Several saddled ones were tied up to the barn, awaiting our inspection.

Like the majority of Russian women, Anna knew next to nothing about horseflesh, so Katie and I studied the tethered animals carefully.

"The grey?" Katie asked.

I shook my head. "No, not the grey. Too small."

"What about the black?"

"Sorry, ewe-necked. Anyway, I think she's in foal."

"Then the brown one?" she wondered. "Can I try that one?"

"Hum, OK, he might do. Yes, by all means try him."

"Does this one have a name?" I called over to Anna. She spoke to Vassily. "His name is Agafon."

Vassily moved away from the barn and walked over to help Katie mount up.

That was when I first saw Count Pompeii and determined to ride him immediately.

Reluctantly, Vassily gave me a leg up. He then jumped onto another horse and shot off across the Russian steppes at a gallop, leaving me to follow as best I could.

Pompeii's head shot up. His small ears turned back and we set off in hot pursuit.

I crouched down in the saddle and gave Pompeii his head. The wind whistled past my ears, Pompeii's hooves drummed on the frozen ground. I hardly dared breathe the sub-zero air which was burning my lungs. My face, the only uncovered part of me, felt like a block of ice. Tears of cold were blurring my vision. My fingers and toes had lost all feeling.

Pompeii didn't care. He required no encouragement from me to over-take Vassily. He was thoroughly enjoying himself.

So was I.

As we passed Vassily, he stared at us in astonishment. I grinned happily at him, then suddenly remembered I was a mother! I turned guiltily to find Katie right on our heels. Her flushed and ecstatic face must have mirrored my own.

"Now we return," announced Vassily, and reluctantly we turned and headed back towards the barn.

"Isn't this amazing?" I said to Katie, as Pompeii pranced beneath me.

"Yes, that was a fantastic gallop," she answered, grinning.

"Look at the steppes all around us – have you ever seen anything so beautiful?"

"It's wonderful. Why don't you choose this horse?" Katie pleaded.

"No, darling, sorry. Look at the way he sticks his nose straight up in the air. Anyway, I have set my heart on this one."

The three of us cantered back to the barn, where Anna was waiting for us, stamping her feet on the frozen ground and smoking irritably. She was cold, bored, impatient, and totally uninterested in horses.

"Keep that stallion away from the mares," she shouted at me.

Oh no, I thought – not a stallion? I couldn't possibly buy a stallion! I had visions of riding a rampant sex-maniac across the whole of Europe.

In addition, there was no way I could keep a stallion once I got home. I had hardly ever seen a stallion in England, where they were considered fearsome, oversexed creatures, to be kept for breeding purposes only.

A mad trip was one thing, but arriving in a sleepy English village with a half-wild stallion was quite another. And yet… despite the voice of reason I knew that I absolutely had to have this little horse that had stolen my heart in one madcap gallop. Something unique had passed between us out there on the snowy steppes. I couldn't define it then and I can't define it now. But whatever it was, I could not ignore it.

But before I had time to say anything, Vassily said something in Russian.

"Do you see anything else you like in the corral?" Anna translated.

We looked over the rails to inspect the herd in the corral. How on earth could one choose from so many? When I looked more closely, however, I realised it would not be too difficult. Several of the mares were obviously in foal. A considerable number of the horses had saddle sores. A few had poor feet. I dismissed about thirty for the simple reason that I did not like the look of them.

Gradually the number of potential candidates grew smaller, until, of the sixty animals in the corral, only a few were left to consider.

"I like that big black mare, and the grey mare next to her, too. Could I take a closer look, please?" I asked

The black one was tall – nearly 16 hands – and raw boned, with very little white on her, and the biggest mouth I have ever seen on a horse. The grey was slightly smaller and finer boned, obviously devoted to her companion, and with a knowing look about her.

I started climbing over the fence. Vassily looked aghast and shouted something incomprehensible.

"Stop!" Anna shrieked. "He says you cannot go in with the horses – those two have never been touched and they're dangerous!" I stopped, unwillingly.

I have been around horses for more than forty years, my dealings with them are entirely intuitive. I liked the look of those two mares: therefore that was good enough reason to buy them. After all, the trip itself was based on instinct, so why not choose the horses on instinct?

Before buying a stallion, I should have discussed it with my husband. I couldn't telephone him, however, because there were no international telephone lines from Alexikovo.

That evening, Katie and I sat down to discuss Pompeii.

"Mummy, obviously it's your decision, but you know it will be very difficult to keep him in England?"

"Yes, Katie, I know there are a load of complications. But I have GOT to have him! After all, he seems very quiet, for a stallion."

"And what about riding him back? What will you do when the mares come into season? Or you meet other mares along the way?"

"I've thought of that, and Anna assures me that Russian mares only come into season in the Spring."

"He will undoubtedly be much more expensive than the mares!"

"Yes, but then stallions always are! And perhaps I can get the money back in stud fees when we get home. And," I was warming to my theme, "I want to cross this breed with English horses, and Arabs, to produce great endurance horses, and what quicker way to bring new blood in than via a stallion?"

The next day we went back to the stud. There we huddled in Vassily's office, a bleak, brown box of a room with scarcely enough room for the four of us, but it had a heater! After half an hour of haggling we had agreed on a price for all three horses – a fortune by Russian standards. The mares were, I considered, reasonably priced, but Pompeii cost five times as much as they did. Although I didn't understand then quite how much over the going rate Vassily was asking, I did realise I was paying a "tourist" price. But Count Pompeii was a very special horse.

So it was that I bought one young stallion and two mares as wild as deer from a man I had never met before.

With the price settled, I turned to the next important issue.

"Vassily, it's now early December, can you get the two mares broken in, and all three horses ready for me to journey back to England next summer?"

I had decided to start the ride in June. Even I was not so crazy as to ride off in the middle of the famous Russian winter. After all, when Napoleon had invaded Russia, he had lost 186,000 horses before winter had really set in.

"*Nyet problyeme!*" he smiled. "But it will be expensive to keep them until the Spring!!"

I didn't know much, but I knew that this was not true. On the other hand, I wanted to be sure all the horses were as well fed as possible.

"OK, I'll leave you some money for food. And keep the mares away from all the stallions! I don't want to come back in June and find they are both in foal!"

Vassily and Anna laughed. "*Nyet problyeme!*"

Almost exactly a year later, I was to remember their blithe assurances with a wry smile.

Before we left the stud, I walked over to say goodbye to Pompeii, who was still tied up to the cart. Patting him on the shoulder, I whispered, "I'll be back soon to rescue you." He looked at me like a fellow conspirator, and suddenly I wondered who was rescuing whom.

CHAPTER 5 – MY ORIGINAL PLAN

At dinner that night we hammered out a rough plan. Vassily, Piotr. Nadyezhda, Anna, Katie and I had been joined by the two Cossacks, the blond Lev and the dark and dangerous Ura Kabil.

With so many visitors, Nadyezhda had produced a rickety trestle and placed it next to the kitchen table. Dozens of vodka bottles materialised from somewhere, the air was thick with the rich scent of stew. Thanks to the excitement, the bitter cold and the fresh air, I was starving and wolfed down whatever was put in front of me. The noise in that tiny kitchen was almost deafening – the men's deep Russian voices, the clatter of cutlery and clink of glasses, the shout of *"Na Zdarovia!"* as yet another toast was drunk.

After the plates were cleared away, cigarettes were lit and I spread out on the table the map of Europe I had brought with me from home, as I had been told that maps in Russia were still a State secret.

"If I go in a straight line, I'll be in the Ukraine after about a month," I said.

"Oh no!! That is impossible! You cannot go into the Ukraine!" Anna and the Cossacks were unanimous.

"Why on earth not?" I was surprised at their vehemence.

"It's well known the Ukraine is full of bandits!"

"Bandits?" I echoed stupidly.

"Yes, bandits. It's not safe for you or the horses. You must go round."

My initial scepticism at their fear faded when I recalled a friend of mine in London who had gone on a business trip to Kiev. "We had to go everywhere in an armoured car, with armed bodyguards," he had told me proudly.

Yes, maybe my Russian hosts were right about their Ukrainian neighbours? In that case, I'd have to move north and ride across Belarus and Poland, and then into Germany.

"You must take a truck," Anna declared briskly.

"Oh, must I?" I replied, disappointed. "What for?"

"You need it for luggage, for tents, for oats, and food for yourself."

"Well, surely a car would do? And anyway, I thought I could buy oats and food along the way."

"No, no. You must take everything with you, and you will need to go across country, off the roads – you must take a truck." Anna was getting more and more bossy. My dream of simply riding a few thousand miles with three horses and a tent was rapidly evaporating.

Although I had used pack camels on my previous trip in Mongolia, it simply never crossed my mind then that I could put all my gear on the mares and ride Pompeii – because pack horses had not been part of the British way of life for more than a hundred years.

So I agreed to take a back-up truck because I did not realise there was an alternative. That would come later. Much later.

Vassily said something to Anna.

"Vassily wants to come with you!" she cried.

"*A ya toje!*" laughed Lev. (So do I!)

Was it the vodka talking? If not, it was wonderful news: it would be a great help to have two Cossacks who knew the horses and were familiar with the area where we were to start.

"In that case," I said, "we must buy Piotr's beautiful mare, Rada, as well!" I didn't want all three of my new horses to be ridden every day: they should have one day off every two or three days. A fourth horse would make this possible. This was translated, and Piotr smiled with pleasure at the thought of my dollars.

Anna was also thinking about money.

"And you'll need a driver" she interjected into my dream, "you can have Arman, a young Kazakh who works in my department."

It was obvious that if I had a truck I would need someone to drive it, but amid the alcohol-fuelled camaraderie of horsemen, Anna's insistence struck a discordant note of "commerce." I did not understand until later – too late – that even the most sophisticated Russians believed in their hearts that all westerners were wealthy and naïve, to be parted from their money as quickly and efficiently as possible.

The next day we took the train back to Moscow, arriving early in the morning, and Katie and I flew out to England a few hours later.

CHAPTER 5 – THE REACTION

As my husband and I were drinking coffee the following morning, I brought up the delicate subject of introducing a semi-wild Cossack stallion into our sleepy village.

To my astonishment, Andrew was thrilled.

"Wonderful! You'll be famous! I can see the TV cameras all over the village as you ride back to the house! But don't be away too long," he added warningly, "how long do you think it will take?"

"Oh, about three months, I should think. Depends on whether any of the horses go lame and I have to wait, or if I have border problems."

The time had come to break the news to my friends.

Their responses varied.

"You're stark staring mad – we'll never see you again."

"Don't be silly, of course you will."

"Don't you know Russia is full of bandits?"

"No more than London."

"How far is it?"

"It's about 2,500 miles."

"I think it's cruel on the horses."

"I've never heard such absolute drivel! This is how horses are supposed to get around!"

"Why don't you bring them back in a horsebox?"

"It never occurred to me. If you bought a car in Russia, would you drive it back, or put it on low-loader? And to box the horses for 2,500 miles, now that *would* be cruel."

"It's an incredibly dangerous undertaking."

I could never understand that argument. Did these people think that if they never ventured out of the cotton-wool packaging of their normal routines, they would live forever? Had none of their friends ever been snatched away by a car crash or cancer? Did they think that if they cowered in their man-made cocoon, Death would never find them?

When I was eight I was nearly killed by my first pony, who threw me off and then tried to disembowel me.

So I had already cheated death once, but I have always known that the Grim Reaper would get me – like everyone else – in the end. And, while I waited, I was going to go out and enjoy life.

What all my English friends wanted to know was: "Why on earth do you want to do this?"

"Er...."

I could not answer the last question, because I honestly did not know. It wasn't that I *wanted* to do it, rather that I felt *impelled* to do it.

Why indeed? I asked myself.

I had a husband, a home, a daughter, two step-sons, horses, dogs, cats, goats, and chickens. I had responsibilities!

But my husband could manage. My home was just a pile of bricks. My faithful gardener/handyman would take care of the animals. The children were grown up.

And I had all the qualifications to undertake such a mad venture. I was a horsewoman. I was a linguist. I was efficient enough to organise the logistics of the journey. I liked people. I was adaptable. And I was determined to succeed.

Why not? I answered myself.

CHAPTER 6 – PLANNING AND PREPARATION

Looking back now, one of the things I instinctively did right was to realise that border crossings would be the biggest problem, and so I began by telephoning the appropriate Government department in Britain.

"What documents do I need to bring horses – a stallion and three mares – into England from Russia?"

The cockney girl working for the Ministry of Agriculture, Fisheries and Food ("MAFF") who had answered the telephone showed no surprise, but I had to wait while she shuffled through some papers.

"They need to have a blood test and a certificate to show they are healthy and free from Dourine, Glanders, and EVA."

Dourine and Glanders were diseases I had vaguely heard of from reading old books about horses, but EVA was new to me.

"What's EVA?"

"Equine Viral Arteritis – it's a sexually-transmitted equine disease. The certificate is valid for ten days," she intoned in an indifferent voice.

"But I'm riding them 2,500 miles – there is no way I can cover that distance in ten days!"

"Then you can't do it," she snapped, and put the receiver down.

This was my first run-in with the bureaucrats. But it was not to be the last.

My proposed journey with Pompeii and his mares was a celebration of ancient equestrian freedom. It ran completely counter to the 20th century obsession with frontiers, rules, safety, anaesthesia and air-conditioned comfort. But I would not be denied: the immovable object of paperwork had just met the irresistible force of a single-minded woman.

I dialled again, and asked to be put through to her boss. He was more helpful, and said that I would need to arrange for the horses to be tested at intervals along the way, the most recent test being within three weeks of arriving at a European Community (EC) border.

"But you have to send the blood to England for testing, we won't accept any foreign certificates," he added.

"Oh no!" I foresaw hideous difficulties. "Why not?"

"Recently an Arab stallion arrived from Poland. He had a paper certifying he was free from EVA. He wasn't! But it was too late. No one found out until after he had covered some of England's best mares. By then they were all sterile. So we can't accept foreign certificates."

"Hmm, I see your point," I agreed reluctantly. "Was the error on the Polish stallion's papers deliberate or just carelessness?"

"We don't know. It doesn't matter!"

Since Germany would be the first EC country we would cross, I sent a fax to the equivalent bureaucrat in Bonn. He sent a response by return. "Please telephone me at once. You cannot across the border ride!! It is not foreseen!!"

I supposed by "not foreseen" he meant "not in the book."

I rang him. My command of the German language, although not brilliant, turned out to be better than his English.

"You can over the frontier with your horses come only if they are in a lorry!" he shrieked.

"Why? Horses are horses, surely it doesn't make any difference to their state of health if they are enclosed in a horsebox or coming across on all four legs?"

He was adamant. "Impossible! It is not permitted across the border to ride!"

I decided to go over his head.

Britain and Germany are two of the countries who make up what was then the European Community (EC), now the European Union, along with virtually every other Western European country. They are all subject, therefore, to the same rules and regulations which have been laid down by the European Parliament which had its headquarters in Belgium.

With some difficulty I acquired the name and telephone number of the Chief Veterinarian in Brussels. Bernard van Goethem was wonderfully co-operative, and talked to both the British and the German authorities, telling them that I was indeed permitted to ride over the border.

"Did you hear about Jean-Louis Gouraud?" Mr. van Goethem added. "He rode from Paris to Moscow in 1990, and it took him three years to arrange!"

"Three years?" I echoed in horror.

"Yes, three years. But you are making your ride at the right moment in history. In the old days, the Soviet regime never allowed anyone to travel in the USSR unless they were accompanied by an Intourist guide. In the future, who knows? The Communists may restore the old system, or maybe Russia will open up so much that it is full of tourists!"

My contact with Bernard van Goethem was to prove to be a Godsend many months later when I ran into a bureaucratic brick wall at my first EC border. The pen-pushers were on the point of shooting my precious Pompeii when Monsieur van Goethem intervened.

In the meantime, my fax machine was humming with messages to and from Moscow.

"Dear Barbara. The Russian vets need to approve your route. I am arranging it now. Love, Anna."

"Dear Anna. Thank you. Why do the vets need to approve my route? Love, Barbara."

"Dear Barbara. They have to be sure you will not get by mistake into Foot and Mouth region. Love, Anna. PS: Small problem. There are no horse shoes in Russia! You must bring your own! Love, Anna."

"Dear Anna. WHAT?? Please can you measure the horses' feet so I can bring the right size shoes?"

"Dear Barbara. I have been to Alexikovo and seen the horses. I have drawn a pencil round the Pompeii's front foot. I attach the drawing."

There on the fax machine was a reminder of my Cossack stallion.

I took the piece of paper to my farrier. "Can you sell me twelve sets of shoes this size? Oh, and I'll need – um – about three hundred nails, please!"

He looked at the drawing.

"Blimey! What are you getting – a herd of carthorses?"

It was true that the pencilled drawing indicated an enormous hoof, and of course there was no guarantee that all the horses would have the same-sized feet, but I had no choice. I came away with 48 shoes – three sets each for the four horses. Thirty-six pounds of raw English iron, plus five pounds of nails. I calculated that these should see us through to Poland.

Meanwhile I applied for a human visa. On the application form, I explained exactly what I was planning to do: go to Moscow to organise the paperwork for the horses, then proceed to *Volgogradski oblast* to pick up the horses, then ride back via Bryansk, Kursk and Smolensk to Belarus.

It didn't matter. When the visa arrived, it was only valid for Moscow. Plus I was surprised to learn that I was going to Russia for the purpose of studying the language!

"Oh well, I expect it'll be OK" I said optimistically, if unwisely, to my husband Andrew.

I had assumed that, in the unlikely event of bandits actually materialising, the Russians would help me. But one morning about a month before my departure I awoke with the cold realisation that I had to be able to take care of myself and protect the horses.

"Andrew, I need to learn self-defence!" I said rather diffidently to my husband one morning. He had contacts in the SAS, otherwise I would have kept my forebodings to myself.

"Are you sure you really want to go through with this lunatic scheme of yours? It is a dangerous undertaking, as you have just admitted."

"Of course I want to do it!" I responded enthusiastically. The last thing I wanted was Andrew telling me not to go! Not that he could have stopped me, but I really did not wish to part on bad terms with him. "I am strong and fit, all I need is somebody to teach me how to fight, should I ever need to. Which I'm sure I won't..." my voice trailed away on the final sentence: even as I spoke, I realised how unconvincing I sounded.

So Andrew found Robin, an ex-SAS soldier who offered courses in self-defence. Nothing fancy: just nasty, vicious street-fighting – perfect! After two days of intensive, one-to-one training, I felt confident I could disable any man.

"Even if I don't encounter a single bandit on the journey," I told Katie, "I feel a lot safer walking round London after dark!"

Finally, after five months of constant preparation, I was ready to leave.

But there was a small problem. Try as I might, I could not keep my luggage down to less than four huge soft nylon bags. They contained:

Horseshoes and nails.

Minimal clothing – for the summer, of course.

Two pairs of boots.

A tent and sleeping bag.

Iron stakes to tether the horses.

No food, of course – I could buy that along the way – but I did take condensed milk and peanuts, both of which pack a lot of calories into a relatively small and light-weight package.

I also carried the barest minimum of cosmetics, just in case I needed to flirt my across a border or some such. But no curling tongs!

I did not take any tack – I planned to buy what I needed when I got down to Alexikovo. The exception to that was headcollars, which are unknown in Russia.

Then there was the small detail of 80lb of vitamin powder for the horses. It was only while packing this that it occurred to me that some sceptical foreign Customs officer along the way was likely to raise his eyebrows at so much unidentified white powder....

The obvious thing to do would have been to fly to Moscow. I thought about the nightmare known as Heathrow Airport, the crowds there, the noise, the stress. Plus I remembered the horrors of landing at Moscow's Sheremetyavo Airport. I looked at my four suitcases (which I mentally referred to as "The Trolls"), and quailed.

I did have one alternative.

Next to horses, my absolute favourite form of transport has always been the train. You rattle through the countryside enjoying the scenery. You converse with exotic strangers in corridors. You sit curled up on a bunk with a good book. You potter down to the dining car. You go to sleep rocked by the lullaby of the clackety-clack of wheels on tracks. There can be no more civilised way to travel!

Could I possibly start my adventure by train? Eurostar would get me from London to Brussels or Paris via the Channel Tunnel, but then what? I could hardly believe it when I discovered there was a daily train from Brussels to Moscow.

"I'll need a one-way ticket from London to Brussels, please," I told the booking clerk over the telephone, "and a one-way ticket from Brussels to Moscow."

"One way? Aren't you coming back?" the puzzled clerk wanted to know.

"Oh yes, but I'm coming back by horse!"

He didn't believe me.

Andrew and I drove to the nearest town to pick up the tickets.

"You really are hell-bent on doing this, aren't you?" he said as we drove along our narrow, winding country roads. I looked around at the comfortable English countryside, unbelievably green as it always is in Spring. Sprays of white hawthorn flowers decorated the hedges, and the fruit trees were in full bloom.

"Of course I am!"

"I really hope it doesn't take too long," Andrew grumbled.

"It shouldn't take more than three months at the outside," I assured him optimistically.   There had been tension between us for several weeks, but I refused to feel guilty that I was, at long last, going off to have fun. I had paid the daily bills for years – now it was Andrew's turn.

With everything packed and with all my other animals taken care of, I left my Wessex village in high spirits on 31st May. Katie hugged me tightly and told me to be careful, the moisture in her eyes revealing her fears. I got in the car before I started crying too, and Andrew pointed the bonnet in the direction of London, and Waterloo Station.

Adventure at last!

I never dreamt it would be six months to the day before my return.

CHAPTER 7 – MY JOURNEY BEGINS

At Brussels station I had a problem. I needed a porter to help me lug "The Trolls" from one station platform to the other. I managed to attract the attention of one porter, tall, fat, with a drooping black moustache, and guessed he was a Flemish-speaker. The simmering dislike between Belgium's French- and Flemish-speakers was even closer to the surface than it had been when I was at school in Brussels aged 12. Unfortunately, the only phrase I could remember from two years studying Flemish was "I am a girl." Why hadn't I memorised the phrase, "I need to catch the Russian train" or even "please can you help me with my bags"?

I was forced to speak to him in French, and before he could turn surly on me, I explained that I was English. *"Oh, très bien, madame"* he said happily, relieved that we had a common language.

Even though he had a large trolley, and I was carrying the smallest Troll, he had a struggle on his hands, and as I followed him along the platform I could hear him puffing and wheezing. Then I saw he was heading for the escalator! Could we get the trolley onto it? Oh yes, this was efficient little Belgium, of course we could. Down we went, along the tunnel below the railway lines, and up the other side. It seemed we had to walk for miles to the Moscow-bound train, but finally we found it. My overweight helper's grumbles turned to a wide smile and "Bon Voyage!" when I tipped him handsomely.

Next I had to enlist the assistance of the Russian train crew to give me a hand to get The Trolls into my cabin. I had bought both berths in a two-bed compartment, so at least I had privacy. Privacy, but not much space: "The Trolls" took up most of the floor space and two-thirds of the lower bunk.

I looked around me. Measuring about seven feet square, the pale grey compartment was spare and utilitarian, but not uncomfortable. There was a window, so I could enjoy the countryside we travelled through, and a tiny hand-basin in the corner beneath it.

As soon as I was settled in, I realised I was absolutely starving after eight hours of travel and exertion.

"Gdye vagon restawran?" (Where's the dining car?) I asked the *provodnik* (attendant) once I had got my breath back.

"Vagon restawran? Nyet! Kanyeshna nyet!" (No, there's no dining car – of course not!)

Oh hell, this means I'm stuck in a tiny compartment on a Russian train and I won't be able to eat for two days!

I had assumed that the train would be a Belgian one, and that there would be a restaurant car, forgetting my late father's invaluable advice, "Never assume!" I was angry with myself for not foreseeing this possibility, got undressed, crawled into the upper bunk, and fell asleep hungry.

At 2.45 a.m. a drumming on the door dragged me from my dreams. I had slept through Germany and we were now approaching the German-Polish border, and soon the train was swarming with Polish Customs men and soldiers. I could hear banging and shouting along the corridor as they searched the slowly-moving train with surprising thoroughness. Then it was my turn – I had barely had time to pull on my jeans and a T-shirt before the door flew open to admit a young soldier in a grey uniform.

"Passport!" he barked at me. His peaked cap slightly askew, he lightly touched the pistol at his belt as he scrutinised my face with exaggerated care and compared it to the photograph in my passport.

His colleague, meanwhile, had squeezed in behind him and was searching every nook of my tiny cabin – even my bed. I wondered what they were looking for. Surely nobody would consider smuggling goods or people into Poland from the West?

The faintly-threatening demeanour of these men left me feeling uneasy – even guilty, although I had nothing to hide – and I was absurdly relieved when they left my cabin, apparently satisfied that I was who I claimed to be. The smell of stale, cheap cigarette smoke hung in the air, as though they had left it behind on purpose to remind me of their power.

The formula was repeated when we crossed from Poland into Belarus about eight hours later. The middle-aged, corpulent and unshaven soldier on duty picked up my heaviest bag in order to look under the seat. Or tried to. He glared at me from underneath his military cap. I gazed steadily back and smiled, hoping against hope that he would not ask me to open it and reveal the bags of suspicious-looking white powder. He didn't. He turned and walked away.

Out of sheer relief that the powder, the nails, The Trolls, tent, horseshoes and gear were all safe, I went to the end of the train to have a cigarette. The soldier who had almost given himself a hernia was there, waiting to get off at the next stop. He smiled at me.

"What is England like?" he asked me in Russian. He was off duty now, and seemed friendly.

"Well, it is very different from Belarus or Russia. England is a small island, crowded. And it rains a lot."

"Oh! How did you get across the sea?" His curiosity was aroused.

"There's a train under the sea from England to France."

"WHAT??" He was absolutely astonished. "How is this possible?"

"There's a tunnel which goes under the floor of the sea," I told him.

He clearly didn't believe my far-fetched tale.

"It isn't very long," I added, "only about forty kilometres"

He stared at me, puffing on his cigarette, and decided to change the subject.

"Don't you know there are bandits in Russia?" he asked, looking genuinely concerned.

"Yes, but there are bandits in England, too." I said yet again, trying to look as though a few bandits were all in a day's work. The last thing I wanted was for some petty official to decide my journey was too dangerous before it even began. Then I remembered I was in Eastern Europe, where nobody would care if I came to a sticky end.

An hour later the train slid into a vast shed, where the carriages had their coupling arrangements changed.

Each individual carriage in turn was lifted 30 feet in the air while new wheels were attached to accommodate a different railway gauge. While we dangled high in the air, the passengers were quite free to wander around the shed and under the carriage. I chose to stay in the train. I stood in the open doorway, watching the workers and passengers far below. One false step would have plunged me to certain death. But no bossy "jobsworths" were on hand to fuss over us or herd us to safety. This was Russia!

We were free to kill ourselves by our own stupidity in any way we chose.

I felt a rush of freedom as I watched this circus of danger.

That evening, the train stopped at a small town and was immediately surrounded by women selling food. Half-dead with hunger, I bought a roast chicken, mineral water, keffir (a thin, yoghurt-type of drink), some beer, went to my cabin and gorged the lot.

Replete at last, I fell into a deep sleep for twelve hours.

At 9 a.m. the following day the train sauntered into Moscow.

CHAPTER 8 - FRUSTRATIONS AND DELAYS IN MOSCOW

Fax from Moscow, 3rd June – Day 1

Dear Andrew

Arrived safely – it's very hot here in Moscow, the hottest summer for over a hundred years, they tell me.

Anna met me at the station with Arman, my driver. I don't like the look of him – he's pleasant enough but he has a spoilt, self-indulgent mouth and I suspect he's a real MCP[1].

Am staying with Vladimir, Anna's father. He's really kind, and has given me his bed while he sleeps in the study. The flat is dreadfully over-furnished and absolutely crammed with books. Unfortunately they are (a) in Russian and (b) all about Sociology!

Hope we can get going in ten days or so. We've decided to get the horses' blood samples tested before we leave – no point in starting if they've got some horrendous disease! Arman will be going down to get the samples as soon as I can find someone to bring them to London. No courier can guarantee the samples won't be left to fry on the runway or freeze in the hold.

Love, Barbara

Fax from Wessex, 4th June – Day 2

Dear Barbara

SO glad you got there in one piece – I was convinced you'd be mugged or raped on the train!

It's hot here, too. All the animals are fine.

Love, Andrew

Moscow, 5th June – Day 3

Dear Andrew

Am absolutely melting. Went to the British Embassy today to see if I could find someone who could bring the horses' blood samples back to Britain. Nice enough people, but they can't help.

Love, Barbara

---

[1] Male Chauvinist Pig!

Moscow, 6th June – Day 4

Dear Andrew

Could you please find out about insurance for the truck? No Russians ever insure anything – lives, houses, cars… But I think we'll need the truck to be insured for Poland, and certainly for Germany and Britain.

Love, Barbara

Wessex, 7th June – Day 5

Dear Barbara

Am getting insurance sorted. Please let me have details of truck: make, model, registration number etc.

Love, Andrew

Moscow, 9th June – Day 7

Dear Andrew

The Number 2 at the British Embassy here has translated my Polish vet. permission into English – seems OK to me. All the Polish authorities require is $100 to let us across the border!

On the way to the Embassy, I got mistaken for a Russian *twice* by men asking for directions! With no make-up and scruffy jeans, I of course don't look like a rich westerner…. Excellent!

Russian improving – reading as much as I can and of course I hear it all around me, which helps. Sadly, Vladimir insists on practising his English – and spends all evening channel-hopping on the TV so I can't get the hang of anything!

Anna will give me truck details tomorrow.

Love, Barbara

Moscow, 15th June – Day 13

Dear Andrew

I've just found out that Anna hasn't even *started* getting British visas for Lev and Arman! I've spoken to someone at the Embassy and don't think it will be a problem, but still, it's another delay.

Have had to pay over $400 for material for the awning which Anna says we'll need to erect next to the truck. Also $110 for a fridge – sorry, darling, this is an awful lot of money for silly luxuries, although the awning might be useful.

The good news is that I've found a helpful member of British Airways staff (Sheila) who is flying to London in a few days and has promised to take the blood samples!! Would you be able to meet her, please, and send the samples to the government laboratories?

Love, Barbara

Wessex, 16th June – Day 14

Dear Barbara

Of course I'll meet Sheila and get the samples off to the lab! Just let me know date, time, flight details and airport. Oh – and tell me what she looks like!

Chechnya is much in the news still – it seems they've taken hundreds of Russian hostages. Is it safe over there? I'm worried!

Love, Andrew

Moscow, 17th June – Day 15

Dear Andrew

Chechnya problem means extra suspicion of foreigners, I suspect, so a nuisance for me. They talk of bombs on the Metro here in Moscow, but the Slav temperament always looks on the gloomy side of everything.

Went to the Moscow Dog Show today – really boring. However, we had a problem with some stupid official who decided not to let us in! We had a pass, a valid pass, but the gatekeeper chose to bar our entry. Anna has taught me how to handle obstinate "jobsworths" like this: stand firm, believe totally that your documents are 100% pukka, then be friendly to the official concerned. She says it is a uniquely Russian problem.

Still unbelievably hot here.

Love, Barbara

Moscow, 18th June – Day 16

Dear Andrew

Terrible news – I am in despair! Arman went down to Alexikovo yesterday to get the blood samples, but it now seems the hired car broke down and he's stuck somewhere. I don't know where, nor even if he was on the way there or back, but I'm dreadfully afraid he won't get them back to Moscow in time for Sheila's flight tomorrow!

If the worst comes to the worst, I'll come back to London myself with the samples – I daren't set off without the all-clear from MAFF.

Love, Barbara

Moscow, 18th June – Day 16

Dear Andrew

All is well!! Arman broke down on the way *back* and finally got into Moscow some time in the middle of the night. I'm dashing off now with Anna to take the samples (suitably labelled in both Russian and English) to Sheila. She is due to arrive at Heathrow Airport at 20.04 hours tomorrow night – she's a tall, pretty blonde. Not much chance of you not noticing her, then!!

Love, Barbara

Moscow, 18th June – Day 16

Dear Barbara

It's just about midnight, but I wanted to let you know that I just got back from the airport, and the samples will go off to MAFF first thing in the morning.

Whatever made you think I'd notice a pretty blonde?!?

Love, Andrew

Moscow, 19th June – Day 17

Dear Andrew

What a relief!! THANK YOU!

I've now discovered what happened with Arman and the hired car. The car broke down on the main road to Volgograd (hundreds of miles of bugger all), but he had no way of telephoning for help. Eventually he managed to flag down a passing lorry and somehow got his car to a garage.

Russia is not in the 20th century when it comes to communications. Arman could not contact Anna to let us know what was going on because he couldn't find a telephone which would make inter-city calls! And no mobile works except in Moscow, because there are no masts.

This means of course that I shall find it very difficult to get word to you after we get going with the horses. Obviously I'll hardly ever find an international telephone, so I'll just have to ring Anna whenever I can and ask her to contact you.

Love, Barbara

England, 21ˢᵗ June – Day 19

Dear Barbara

Good news! Both mares have passed their dourine and glanders tests.
The EVA test for Pompeii takes four days, so we won't know the result
for another couple of days.

Katie is home for the weekend, and sends you her love.

Love, Andrew

Wessex, 23ʳᵈ June – Day 21

Dear Barbara

Pompeii has passed his EVA test! So perhaps you can leave at the
end of next week?

You know, you are almost excessively brave, but this is such a dangerous undertaking - I am really worried about your safety. I may add
that most of your friends here fear they'll never see you again.

Love, Andrew

Moscow, 24ᵗʰ June – Day 22

Dear Andrew

Oh tosh! For God's sake, don't worry about me. You know I am not
foolhardy, and you know also that I would never wantonly risk the
horses' lives. After all, just hacking round the Wessex roads is
hazardous!

Delighted to hear Pompeii has got a clean bill of health. But we can't
leave yet – it now seems that nobody at the Belarus Embassy here in
Moscow knows what the form is about crossing into Belarus on horses.
This means I may have to go to Minsk!

The bureaucratic hurdles seem endless – never mind leaving at the
end of next week, the way things are going here we'll be bloody lucky if
we get going by the end of next *month*. I haven't even got the visas for
the Russians yet, either!

By the way, I think perhaps we ought to have something in writing
from Bernard van Goethem to the effect that I can *ride* into the EEC?
Would you mind having a word with him, please? Then I'll be able to
wave a piece of paper at any bumptious border official!

Please give my love to Katie.

Love, Barbara

Moscow, 26th June – Day 24

Dear Andrew

We seem to be getting somewhere, at last. I've spoken to the Head of the Visa Section at the British Embassy who has kindly said we can jump the queue. The possible bad news is that they may want to see Lev. I pointed out that (a) he has a wife and children, and a job, so was certain to return to Russia, and (b) it would take ten hours for him to travel to Moscow for an interview.

This is all particularly irritating as Anna had assured me the British visa situation had been dealt with!

She is driving me mad – all she ever seems to do is play on her computer at work and come up with new ways of parting me from my money – but there is not much I can do about it.

We are also still waiting for permission from the Russian vets, who have to approve our route. I thought THAT had been dealt with months ago, too.

Love, Barbara

Moscow, 28th June – Day 26

Dear Andrew

Well, Anna, Arman and I just got back from the British Embassy. The chap we saw there was willing to issue the visas without interviewing Lev, although he did remark that I "had a lot of trust in these two young men."

As far as the vets are concerned, it seems that the vets in Alexikovo and Volgograd need to agree something before the Moscow vets can proceed – and *vice versa*!! Talk about Catch-22.... Frankly, I am tearing my hair out. All I want to do is ride some horses a couple of thousand miles. However did they manage in the old days?

By the way, I had to go and buy a few things today. You cannot imagine what a saga shopping is here! You start by going to the appropriate counter. If you want cheese, for example, it is cut and weighed and you are told the price. Then you might want some vegetables, so you go to the vegetable section.

You work your way round the shop like this, ordering your purchases from each individual counter, until you have ordered everything you need.

Then you join the queue at the cash desk and tell the cashier exactly what you want, e.g. "1.5 kilos of cheese – 18 roubles, 1 jar of tomatoes, 8 roubles, 2 loaves of bread, 5 roubles each, 1 bottle vodka, 10 roubles," and so on.

The cashier rings it all up and gives you one receipt for each set of purchases, so you meekly return to each counter, hand over the receipt and are given your cheese, tomatoes, vodka, etc. etc.

Can you imagine shopping like that every day? I had to make notes on my list, otherwise I would never have remembered the exact price of everything!

Love, Barbara

Wessex, 30th June – Day 28

Dear Barbara

I have at last succeeded in tracking Bernard van Goethem down – I've just received a fax (copy attached) saying that "it is clear the horses may come into the EC on foot – yes"!

Love, Andrew

Moscow, 3rd July – Day 31

Dear Andrew

More bad news on the money front, I'm afraid. Lev is disappointed at the delay and now says he wants $500 to ride to England with me. Is there no end? Anna says there's a meeting with the vets tomorrow. I am beginning to think I'll never get out of Moscow – it is so frustrating!

Love, Barbara

Moscow, 5th July – Day 33

Dear Andrew

I am literally in a state of shock! Anna calmly announced this morning that I have to pay $3000 tomorrow for the truck and Arman, that she wants $3500 for her "work," the vets will charge $1000, $1000 to Nikolai Bezbatka, one of her colleagues, who has promised to help us across the border into Belarus! On top of all that I need to allow $4000 emergency money for the trip, plus $600 for food and equipment, and $600 for petrol as far as the Polish border.

I am absolutely bloody furious - I have asked Anna over and over again how much to budget for, to no avail, and now she hits me with a bill for nearly $15,000.

I could weep.

Love, Barbara

Wessex, 6th July – Day 34

Dear Barbara

She's stitched you up!!

Ring ITN[2] in Moscow – Julian Manyon. They want to film your departure!

Love, Andrew

Moscow, 10th July – Day 38

Dear Andrew

I've spoken to Julian, and he's very interested! I'm to let him know details, dates etc. when I know what's going on.

Anna is worried about nuclear fall-out after Chernobyl, so we've bought a map that shows the most dangerous parts, and a Geiger counter! I also spoke to the British Ambassador's office in Minsk, and their advice was, "It's not bad. Avoid mushrooms, fruits of the forest and dairy products." Fine – how am I supposed to stop the horses from eating grass at night?!

Love, Barbara

Moscow, 14th July – Day 42

Dear Andrew

I do believe we might be getting somewhere – or am I just being stupidly optimistic? We have the visas for the Russians, my Belarus visa, and permission from the Moscow vets. Since the only bureaucratic barrier left is a document from the Volgograd vets, I've suggested to Anna we could leave at the weekend.

I've made a list of lessons I have learnt!

1.   However wildly expensive you think it's going to be – double it.

---

[2] Independent Television News

2.   Don't EVER try and get animals across borders – the paperwork is too daunting.

3.   Get everything in writing!

I've just been interviewed by ITN, and they plan to come down and film our departure.

Love, Barbara

Moscow, 17th July – Day 45

Dear Andrew

I saw the "truck" today for the first time – I was horrified to see that it is nothing more than a van! Well, that puts paid to any idea of going across country. I could scream – but it's too late to change anything now.

We'll be going down to Alexikovo tomorrow. I just can't *wait* to see Pompeii again and to get back in the saddle. Can you believe I've been sweltering in Moscow for FORTY-FIVE DAYS?

I'll contact you whenever I can, but don't forget the lack of international lines! So you mustn't worry if you don't hear from me for a while, I'll be fine.

Love, and thanks again for your support. Barbara

Wessex, 17th July – Day 45

Dear Barbara

Please, please be careful! I shall be worried sick while you are travelling, especially if I don't hear from you for long periods.

Look after yourself, brave girl.

Love, Andrew

CHAPTER 9 – VOLGOGRAD COUNTY

"WHAT?"

"We think it is safer for you to travel with Vassily." Anna seemed quite taken aback at my reaction, obviously unaware that any English-woman asked to share a two-berth compartment with a completely strange man would be outraged. "Your tickets are for different carriages, but maybe we can change them."

It had been decided that Arman and Anna should drive down to Alexikovo, leaving me to take the train with Vassily Teryentitch, the second driver. I had met him the day before we left, which of course would have left me no time to say I didn't like him and wanted another. As it was, my first impression had been of a kindly old man. Vassily was in his sixties, stocky and dependable-looking, with white hair and gentle blue eyes. He shook my hand, said *"Zdrastvoytye"*, and smiled.

I am not one of those women who live in constant fear of rape. Even if I had been, nobody could have looked less predatory than dear, avun-cular Vassily. I decided therefore to accept whatever Anna had planned, odd though it seemed.

As we had loaded all the luggage and equipment into the van, Vassily and I only had an overnight bag each. Fighting our way through the crowds at the *Vagzall* was not difficult, and I soon found my compart-ment.

"Dobry vyecher" (good evening), I said politely to a very smartly-dressed, 50-year-old woman with dyed black hair who was already installed on one of the bunks. Anna was pushing me from behind so I stood aside to let her in. A deluge of Russian ensued, with Anna trying her utmost to persuade the woman to exchange bunks with Vassily. The lady would not be moved, however, and so rather to my relief it was finally settled that I should share the compartment with her.

We made ourselves comfortable and settled down to chat. Tamara, I discovered, was recently widowed and was on her way to visit her mother in Alexikovo. But she was wildly curious about me – I was the first foreigner she had ever met! In answer to her barrage of questions I told her about my home, my husband, my daughter. I explained how I had bought some horses and was going to ride them back to England.

"But what a wonderful thing! How long will it take you?"

"Oh, three months, I think."

"How far is it?"

"I'm not sure, about 2,500 miles – that's 4,000 kilometres."

Just as last time, the train pulled into Alexikovo early in the morning, and Anna and Piotr were there to meet me.

Anna was in a very bad-tempered mood, and opened the conversation by announcing that I had to pay tax of $225 per horse. "Not yet *more* unexpected expenses?" I groaned. "It is necessary" she snapped as she held the front seat forward so I could crawl into the rear seat next to Vassily.

My two previous visits to Piotr and Nadyezhda's house had not prepared me for the overwhelming summer stench which assailed my nostrils as soon as I stepped out of the car. The yard was full of young creatures – puppies, kittens, and calves, not to mention dozens of little chickens, turkeys, guinea-fowl and Muscovy ducks. I enquired about Rada, the beautiful iron-grey mare I had chosen on my last visit, so Piotr led the way into one of his dilapidated sheds. There I found Rada, chained up in the most disgusting filth. Somehow she had transformed herself into a strawberry roan, and looked magnificent, in spite of her surroundings.

After a quick lunch I asked if we could go and see Pompeii and the two other mares. With very bad grace, Anna agreed, and she, Piotr and I clambered back into the little car and drove to Vassily Vadianov's house rather than to the stables. The grey, who had apparently been named "Malishka," was nowhere to be seen, but Pompeii and the black mare were tied up together, drowsing in the heat, on long chains in an open-sided shed.

I walked towards them. "*Astarojna!*" (Be careful!) Vassily called out, and spoke rapidly to Anna. "Vassily says you cannot trust the black one," she warned. That's nice, I mused. I paid a fortune for the horses and left a ton of money for their food and training. Now you tell me one of them is dangerous!

But I said nothing, just walked to the other side of the hut and went to stroke and chat to Pompeii. He looked at me sleepily, and accepted my caresses as nothing less than his due. He was as skinny as ever.

I refused to be cowed by the black horse – after all, we would be travelling together for weeks – and walked back around to talk to her. Vassily had exaggerated her fierceness, as she paid no attention at all when I approached her carefully and patted her neck.

"What's her name?" I called out.

"Masha"

"How confusing, that's very like Malishka!"

Anna laughed. "Actually it's the same name – one a diminutive of the other – the Cossacks just couldn't be bothered to think of another one!"

Vassily took us into his house, where we were welcomed by his wife, Tatiana. Short, dyed red hair the consistency of straw clashed horribly with a purple and orange floral dress, and half her teeth were gold, but her hospitality was of the warmest. I put her at about 45, but later Anna told me that she and Vassily were trying for a baby. "At her age?" I had exclaimed. "Why not? She's 32."

We still had some final documents to obtain from the vets and Customs. At least, I hoped they were the final documents. So we left the Vadianov home and spent two and a half hours in the vet's office in Alexikovo. Why was I not surprised to learn then that the Volgograd vets also had to sign this important piece of paper? It was agreed that we would get up at 4 a.m. the next day so as to get to Volgograd by 8 a.m.

I struggled out of bed at 4.15, but after we had waited for Anna to have some bread and tea and heat up a pan of soup to give us strength for the journey, it was nearly 6 a.m. before we set off. Arman was our driver this time, and although he drove very fast it took four hours to get to Volgograd.

We went into the vet's office. "At last somebody recognises the value of our working horses!" he cried, delighted to hear about my journey. He signed the necessary papers immediately.

"Now we have to go to another vet," Anna declared.

"Whatever for?"

"Two vets have to sign the documents."

By now I thought nothing the bureaucrats did or demanded could surprise me. I was wrong: there was a long and heated exchange between Anna and the second vet before she stormed out.

"What's happening?" I asked as I trotted beside her to the car.

"This vet says we must fill in a form to say the horses must not be inoculated against Anthrax."

"That's crazy!"

"Yes, so now we go back to the first vet, who is nice. Maybe he will help us."

The first vet seemed as exasperated as we were and telephoned his colleague to tell him not to be so silly. We rushed back to the difficult vet's office where, after keeping us waiting for two hours, he reluctantly gave us one of the two documents we needed.

By now it was just after 3 p.m. We still had to get a certificate from the Customs office, which is normally open until 5 p.m. That day they had chosen to close at 3 p.m.

I was very angry and deeply depressed.

"Anna, what is the point in getting all these documents?"

"They are necessary, without them you will have big trouble."

"But it seems impossible to get them! And then, even if we *can* get them, anybody in authority can challenge us and refuse to accept them as valid!"

"This is how it is, Barbara. You have to have every possible document and then be ready to discuss it with anybody who tries to stop you."

By the time we got home it was very late and we were all exhausted. Word of my arrival had spread among the Cossack community, however, and Ura Kabil appeared at supper time, looking very dashing on a motorcycle. He hugged me tightly, as though we were old friends, and suddenly it seemed like only yesterday that he had given me the Cossack whip and bridle. Then Lev turned up too. The sun had bleached his blond hair almost white.

We all crowded into the kitchen for supper and Nadyezhda put a delicious meal of kebabs on the table. As the others talked, I stripped the meat off the skewers, and wondered why I was having such trouble understanding the locals. When Piotr, Ura, or Lev spoke directly to me, it was fine, but when they spoke among themselves I was lost. This evening I listened intently, and realised that I kept hearing one word over and over again.

"Anna, what does *xooee* mean?" It was an innocent-enough question, and I was a little taken aback when everyone around the table exploded in mirth. When Anna had stopped laughing, she dried her eyes. "It means the same as 'fuck' in your language," she giggled.

So that was it!

From then on I had very little difficulty: once I realised that that word could safely be ignored, the rest of the sentence made perfect sense!

We explained to Ura the trouble we were having with the vets and the Customs, and how nearly impossible it seemed to get the exact documents that were required.

"I may be able to help," he winked at me, "my cousin works for the Customs and I'll talk to him."

Ura was as good as his word. Two days later he reappeared and suddenly we had everything we needed. We could leave!

In the meantime, Vassily and I had ridden Pompeii, Masha and Malishka from his place to Piotr's.

How happy I was to get back in the saddle!

How insufferable was the heat.

How the flies tortured us.

Poor Pompeii suffered the most – a type of fly I had never seen before seemed particularly attracted to the stallion's testicles, driving him mad. I resolved then and there that on the trip we would get up before dawn and ride as far as possible in the early-morning cool.

"Vassily, *shto eta?*" (what is it?) I asked, pointing to the flies clustered around Pompeii's genitals.

"*Eta ovd*[3]," he replied. "*Ploxa*" (bad).

"*Da, ochin ploxa!*" I agreed. (Yes, very bad.)

Eventually we trotted into Piotr's yard, and the three horses were tied up to a cart full of the most wonderful hay. In the evening we took them to the village pump – no running water here. Pompeii refused to drink, and I thought of the old English proverb, "You can take a horse to water, but you can't make him drink," and realised that of course there was a time in England when people had no plumbing. Unimaginable nowadays!

I studied the four horses carefully. They were all dreadfully scarred, and had signs of old saddle-sores, which was appalling. After all the oldest one, Pompeii, was only five. On top of that, Rada had just acquired a horrible wound on her shoulder.

"I think that needs stitching," I said to Anna. She consulted Piotr.

"No, Piotr says it is not necessary. He will give you powder to put in it."

Apart from that, we were ready.

---

[3] Gadflies

The television crew had come down from Moscow to film my departure.

It was nearly two months since I had left England.

CHAPTER 10 – WE LEAVE, AND THE CREW GOES ON STRIKE

"It is very strange, Barbara," my Cossack friend Ura said as we cantered along side by side across the Russian steppes at the start of my journey. "I am a communist and you are a capitalist, but now I realise that we are both just people!"

"Ura, I am not a capitalist! "

"Yes, yes, you must be, you are English."

My command of the Russian language was not yet adequate to protest that I was definitely not a fully-paid-up member of the Capitalist Party, so I just smiled at him. Yet his observation was spot on: in spite of years of brainwashing on both sides of the Iron Curtain, we two had found out that the chap on the other side of that curtain was nothing more threatening than a fellow human being.

More than that: Ura and I had discovered something else, another universal bond – we were horsemen. The age-old relationship between humans and equines had brought this communist Cossack and spoilt European together in total harmony. It mattered not one whit that he had lived his entire life in one tiny Russian village, while I had spent years travelling around Europe in a first-class train. The fact that I could ride was better than a passport as far as he was concerned, and *vice versa*.

Ura and Vassily Vadianov's brother, also called Ura, had decided to accompany Lev and me for a couple of days. So we four horsemen had jumped in the saddle, while Piotr and Anna climbed into Piotr's car, and Arman and Vassily got into the van.

The whole village turned out to see us off, there were kisses, hugs and jubilation all round. A toast was drunk (of course!) and off we went.

I rode Pompeii as we cantered westwards. Everyone was in high spirits, laughing and joking. I could hardly believe that my dream was actually beginning, after all the work, the research, the documents, delays, and disappointments.

We were heading for England, at last!

And my real troubles were about to begin.

My Cossack companions, who had assured me they all knew the way, started stopping local people to ask directions, then disagreeing among themselves about the correct route. We rode through beautiful woods along lovely tracks, far from any roads.

This was my first experience of riding through a huge country.

It's humbling. You breast a rise and can see for fifty miles ahead, and you realise that it will take you more than a day to get to the horizon.

We had wasted a lot of time and energy showing off for the cameras, so the horses, who were too thin and hopelessly unfit, had a bad time that first day. We did not arrive at the campsite (chosen, of course, by Anna) until 9 p.m. After tethering and feeding the horses, I put up my tent, ready for supper and bed. The Russians had an agenda of their own, however, and sat around smoking and talking and arguing until 11 p.m., when I gave up, grabbed a piece of bread and a slice of salami, and went to bed.

I was angry, but could see no point in quarrelling with Anna. She was in a foul mood already, and shouting at everyone, and soon she'd be gone and I would be able to take charge. Or so I thought.

Pompeii had been as sensible as ever, and his two mares (Malishka and Masha) had been well broken in. I was pleased with my choices. Rada, however, was another matter. She had become extremely bad-tempered since I had selected her, and was liable to bite and kick humans and her fellow-equines with equal venom. She'd better mend her ways, I thought. We all needed to be friends, and I didn't fancy being kicked into the middle of next week when trying to feed her.

Day Two was hardly an improvement.

The horses were in good form at first. Only Ura Kabil felt like riding, so I rode Rada and Ura climbed on board Masha, with Pompeii tied to the back of black Masha's saddle. Grey Malishka, who had already shown herself to be devoted to her black friend, was allowed to run free, and she never left our side.

Although Russians frequently tie the led horse to the rear hoop of their saddles, I was not happy with the arrangement. Rightly so, as it turned out – in a desperate effort to rid himself of a cloud of gadflies as we travelled along the edge of a dense wood, Pompeii got down and rolled, thereby breaking the reins.

"No more!" I cried, dismounting. I mended the rein with a piece of string, and got back in the saddle with Pompeii's rein in my hand.

I had difficulties immediately. Pompeii absolutely hated Rada, and was afraid he might be kicked. I encouraged him to come up level with my leg, rather than walk behind us as the Russians normally do. It helped.

Ura, who had been told where we were supposed to meet our crew, gradually started veering off in the wrong direction. At first I said nothing, thinking he must know the way, but when we had almost completed a circle I called out to him.

"Ura! *Padajdee!* (wait!)" I called. "Look, we are going there" and I pointed east-north-east, "when we should be going *that* way" and pointed west.

"*Nyet! Nyet! Eta xarasho!*" (No, no, this is right!) Ura insisted.

"No, it is *wrong*." I said. The last thing I wanted was to go for miles in the wrong direction and tire the horses unnecessarily. To make matters even worse, the sky was darkening rapidly as a massive black cloud moved inexorably towards us.

As we argued, Piotr and Anna came tearing up in their little car, shouting and screaming that we were going the wrong way. At that moment the heavens opened and in three seconds we were all completely drenched.

So, on only the second day we covered sixty-five kilometres, far too much for my poor unfit horses. Masha was exhausted by the time we rode into camp, having carried a heavy man both days. I was livid, but said little because Anna and the other hangers-on were to leave after supper that evening. I anticipated being in control of both distance and speed from then on.

"Barbara, goodbye, good luck!" Anna hugged and kissed me. "Let me know how you get on."

"Of course I will, Anna. I shall ring you whenever I can."

"*Do svedanya!*" (goodbye) echoed Piotr and the two Uras. "*Schesleevova Pooti!*" (Bon voyage). Ura Kabil kissed me on both cheeks and gave me a crucifix for luck. "Take it," he urged, "it belonged to my mother."

I fell into bed, exhausted. When I crawled out of my tent the following morning, the men were waiting for me.

"*S dnyom rajdyenia!*" (Happy birthday!)

I had forgotten it was my birthday! The men crowded round me, offering gifts. Lev handed me a bunch of dandelions and a packet of Russian cigarettes, while Vassily gave me a box of matches. This being Russia, naturally we had to have a shot of vodka each.

We switched horses again, and I rode Pompeii and led Masha, while Lev rode Malishka and led Rada. This brought another difficulty –

Malishka was afraid of being bitten by Rada, and kept throwing nervous glances over her shoulder.

Across the beautiful countryside we went again, but my crew revealed themselves to be completely incompetent. Arman and Lev muttered in low voices about where we should meet up next, but more often that not when we arrived at the appointed rendezvous, there would be no sight of the van. More by luck than good judgement we did see the van at about lunchtime, waved frantically, and were reunited.

"Arman, I think the horses need a long rest now, they are tired," I suggested. "This is a good place, as there is plenty of grass."

"OK." Was I imagining it, or was Arman sulking? He certainly looked very sullen.

"And, Arman, do you think it would be a good idea if Lev and I stayed a bit closer to the road? That way it will be easier for you to see us."

"Yes, yes, very good idea."

He studied the map, and we agreed to make camp about six or seven kilometres further on.

The map! How I came to loathe that map! It was a road atlas, on a scale of 1:2,500,000 or even 1:3,000,000, and completely unsuited to our needs. It did not show the smaller roads – the ones we wanted to use. Yet again I had been fooled. Although I had known that until *Perestroika* all maps of Russia were secret documents, I had been assured by one of Anna's colleagues at the Moscow Academy of Sciences that he would find us a good one.

By the end of the day I was furious again. We trudged along not for six kilometres, as Arman and I had agreed, but about fifteen before Lev and I found a reasonable campsite. The van was nowhere to be seen, so we sent up a flare. A few minutes later Vassily and Arman drove up.

The camp was well hidden from the road behind a thick belt of trees, so we tied the horses up in this screen and gave them oats and some sweetcorn we had grabbed from a field. Only at nightfall did we dare bring them into the open grassland behind the trees and put them on their long tethers.

The simmering resentment the men all felt exploded that night. What a birthday!

"There are not enough people," complained Arman. "If you and Lev ride all day, you must sleep at night. We are tired, too, so cannot stay awake to keep watch."

"Well, if we do need to keep watch, we must change the routine," I replied. "If you and I agree where we are to meet each evening, you and Vassily can drive there and rest all day. And why don't you buy a can of paint? That way you can leave a sign by the road to show us where you are."

Lev spoke rapidly to Arman.

"Lev says, it is dangerous to ride where we can be seen from the road, and we should have four riders."

"That's ridiculous!" I cried. "Why is it dangerous? We don't need more riders – two riders can easily manage four horses!"

"It's dangerous because people from the road might see you and follow you."

"What for? We don't look like rich Westerners, for heaven's sake! Why would they need to follow us?" I was getting irritated by their fearful attitude. If they thought it was so perilous to do this, why on earth had they agreed to come and "help" me?

"Barbara, you don't understand. Look at those boots on your feet. Some man who urgently needs a bottle of vodka would kill you for those boots, sell them, and get his alcohol that way."

"Oh for goodness sake! I've never heard anything so silly," I retorted. "But OK, we'll go and talk to the police and see if they can help us in some way."

Lev muttered something again.

"Lev says Malishka is not moving properly, we need to find a vet."

Lev had said this to me earlier in the day, but although I checked her very carefully, I could find no lameness, no heat, and no swelling. The grey had obviously had less practice at being tethered, and several times she had got tangled up in the rope and panicked. Masha was much better, while Pompeii behaved for all the world as though he had spent his life on the road. Even when the rope did wind itself round one of his feet, dear Pompeii just stood there waiting for me to sort him out.

Rada was obviously also accustomed to being tethered. She continued to be very aggressive, however, and loathed the other horses as much as they hated her. I foresaw difficulties.

The very next day my fears were confirmed. I was on Masha, while Lev was riding Rada, and neither of the other horses would consent to be led behind her, for fear of being kicked.

"Lev, I'll lead both horses," I said.

"You can't possibly do that – it's much too dangerous!"

"Well, we have no choice. And I don't think it is too dangerous as long as I'm careful."

We were heading for a small town called Butulinovka, and shortly before we reached it we halted, untacked and tethered the horses and left Vassily and Lev to keep an eye on them while Arman and I went in search of the police station. There didn't seem to be one, but on the other side of town we found a building belonging to *GAI* (traffic police). Young, spotty, unhealthy-looking louts strutted around, waving their Kalashnikovs around and smoking on duty. When we told them our far-away destination, they looked unimpressed. At the time I assumed they thought it beneath their dignity to look surprised. Later on I came to understand that most rural Russians have never heard of England, and I never met a single one who knew where it was.

The *GAI* police did have the grace, however, to draw a plan for us, showing how we could get round the town off the asphalt. And in answer to a question from Arman, they assured us that there were no gypsies in the area who might try to steal my horses.

We returned to the others and mounted up again. The horses had recovered from the first couple of days. Unfortunately, as the equines gradually grew fitter, the humans became more morose. Lev maintained a stony silence as we rode along the dirt-track round town, and after a couple of hours of travelling up hill and down dale in incredibly hot and dusty conditions, I realised he had no idea where to go. Luckily, I had heard Arman shout a last-minute instruction as we had set off, "If all else fails, we'll meet at the *GAI* station!"

"Lev, we must go down there," I pointed. "The *GAI* is at the bottom of this hill." Lev threw me a filthy look, but followed me to the station. There we waited for forty minutes before the others drove up in the van, all hot and bothered.

"We have been looking for you everywhere!" Arman shouted accusingly.

"Well, we just rode round town as agreed," I replied calmly.

"But we couldn't find you!"

"Well, we're all together now, we waited for you here just as you suggested." Really, the man was completely incompetent!

Worse was to come.

"Have you found a good place to camp?" I enquired.

"No!"

"Um – why not, Arman?"

"Because we didn't have time."

I looked at his fleshy, sulky, self-indulgent brown face and thought how ironic it was that I was completely stuck with the first person I had ever really disliked in my entire life.

"Oh really, Arman, you could have been looking for a campsite instead of wasting petrol driving uselessly all over town looking for us!"

"But, Barbara, you need protection!" he wailed. "And there are too many people living round here – it will get harder and harder to find places to camp."

We found a perfectly good place to make camp in a beautiful orchard, and the horses were tethered as usual. The men lit a fire and started whispering together while I took each horse his ration of oats. What were they plotting now, I wondered, narrowly escaping being bitten by Rada as I approached with her bucket. *"Foo!"* (Don't!) I shouted at her.

After a supper of packet soup, which was hardly adequate considering we had had nothing to eat all day, we sat round the camp fire, listening to the crickets chirruping away while the smell of ripening apples drifted down from the trees.

Now the men, my so-called back-up team, were in open rebellion.

"We are going too slowly!" grumbled Vassily.

"What do you mean?" I asked.

"Nikolai Bezbatka" (one of Anna's colleagues at the Academy of Science) "told us that you'd be covering 120 kilometres a day. You're only doing about fifty or sixty."

"What? No way could we ever expect to do 120 kilometres a day – not day after day. Nikolai doesn't know anything about it, anyway, he's not a horseman. But now the horses are fitter, we can move faster and gradually work up to maybe eighty kilometres a day – some days. But Lev refuses to trot, so that is slowing us down badly."

They all looked a little sheepish.

"You cannot go faster," Arman asserted.

"Why not? You've just complained we're going too slowly!"

"Lev hurts."

"What – his bottom?"

"Yes."

"But why? He's a Cossack, for heaven's sake!" I could not believe what Arman was telling me. A saddle-sore Cossack?

"I know. But he hasn't ridden for ten years."

"You're joking?"

"No. He thought there would be three horsemen, so two of them could take it in turns to ride."

This was too much.

"Arman, let me tell you something.

I paid a lot of money for the horses to be made fit. They weren't.

Thanks to Anna we rode too far and too fast for the first few days.

Now we are ready to move faster, and you tell me that Lev is saddle-sore. He knew we were riding about four thousand kilometres, why on earth didn't he go and get himself fit?

Finally, if Anna thinks we have enough people, then what are you worrying about?

Look, I am more than willing to hurry up, but none of these problems we have been having are my fault, so don't look daggers at me! Did you think this trip would be some kind of a picnic?"

I stalked off to see if the horses were all right before I went to bed. It was lucky I did so – dear, dreamy Pompeii had wrapped his tether around a tree and was stuck. I set my alarm as usual for 02.30 so I could inspect the horses then, and crawled into my tent.

After my 02.30 check I could not go back to sleep, so I sat on a log in the dark, smoking and trying to decide what to do. Rada would have to go, I concluded reluctantly. She was probably the best-looking one of the bunch, and certainly the fittest, but I could not continue with a renegade like her.

Lev would have to go too. Apart from his saddle-sores, which would presumably heal in due course, he was obviously extremely unhappy and terrified of bandits.

Arman was not much use, but I needed him.

Vassily was also useless, but at least he was kind.

I had to be ruthless if I was to succeed, but I hated being forced into a position of having to be so assertive.

I felt better after making some decisions, and woke everyone up at 5.45 a.m. Getting the Russians going in the morning was a daily nightmare. They woke up readily enough, but left to their own devices they would have spent three hours drinking tea, eating, and chatting. Over breakfast I told them of the decisions I had made. Lev was delighted, but Arman thought we might have difficulty finding someone to take Rada.

It was getting light, so I started tacking up the two riding horses.

"We can't leave now!" Arman exclaimed in horror. "It's foggy and much too dangerous to ride on the road."

"Yes," agreed Lev and Vassily. "Very risky."

"No it isn't dangerous at all," I said, rather sharply. "There is a little early-morning mist, which means it will be a hot day, and the verge beside the road is ten metres wide."

In spite of their complaints, I succeeded somehow in getting them on the road before 8 a.m.

We plodded along the roadside, inching our way across the map at a snail's pace. I began to think it would take a year to get home, so vast were the distances involved.

At lunchtime Arman and I went to telephone Anna.

"You *must* take Rada, otherwise you will have problems with Customs because your document shows you have four horses!" she shrieked.

"Sorry, Anna, I can't take that horse."

"You will need another rider – I can arrange it – it is just a question of payment…."

I had of course realised that I really ought to have another rider, but I had already paid Lev to do the whole journey and would have been disinclined to shell out more money for somebody else to do the job even if I had had limitless funds. I decided to get rid of Rada at the earliest opportunity, then press on alone for a while.

The biggest danger of riding alone with three horses is not the horses themselves, nor even the traffic. It is the terrain. One person and three horses means there must always be at least two horses abreast, but there were so many traps and dangers to look out for! Rusty old iron and discarded farm or garden implements were strewn along the verges, not to mention occasional huge holes, empty vodka bottles and, in the villages, the ropes of innumerable goats and cows tethered by the roadside.

Although Malishka would never stray far from Masha's side, I did not dare leave her running loose when we were close to a road. And I had given up expecting Arman to find me unless we were beside a road.

We were approaching a town called Liski, and I was determined to get help there. I asked Arman to drive me into Liski and find a lawyer, as I had resolved to "sell" Rada to Lev. I reasoned that the document-loving Russian authorities at the border would be quite happy to see only three horses if I had a piece of paper to "prove" I had sold one of them along the way.

We were in totally different country by now. The landscape had changed from undulating steppes to steep hills, and the rich loam of Alexikovo had been replaced by sandy soil. As I rode, the scent of conifers wafted around me, making me quite homesick for Switzerland, where I was born. Arman even managed to find a really good place to camp.

I was really tired. I was getting up at 05.30, giving the horses their oats, taking down my tent, having breakfast, goading the crew into activity, tacking up, mounting up, riding all day, searching for a campsite, unsaddling, tethering and feeding the horses before having something to eat myself. By then it was never earlier than 10 p.m. At 02.30 I would get up to check the horses, then at 05.30 another day would start.

I had decided before we set off from Alexikovo that the horses should have one day off a week. As we had now found a really good camp not far from Liski, I resolved to give the horses a rest, and use that day to go and find a lawyer and try and find someone to take Rada.

"OK, Arman, let's go!" I climbed in the van with Arman, leaving the other two to watch over the horses.

"It will be very difficult," Arman moaned.

"Tosh!"

"What?"

"Sorry, that's an old-fashioned English expression. It means 'rubbish'. I do not think it will be too difficult, really."

In Liski we discovered, amazingly, a Customs office, so we marched in. Well, I marched in with Arman trailing unwillingly behind me. He spoke to the very nice woman in charge there, explaining our problem with Rada.

"Where is this woman going?" she asked.

"To England."

"Really? How wonderful! *Smyelly jenshina!*" I was embarrassed by her comment ("brave woman") so pretended I did not understand.

"But we need to get rid of one of the horses and the documents we obtained from Customs in Volgograd and Ooryoopinsk all state that this English woman has four horses. Will that be a problem?"

"No, no, no problem. It would be a problem if she had one *more* horse, no problem with one *less*. What are you going to do with the horse you don't want?"

"We don't know. Perhaps we can sell her."

"Why don't you try the local stables? They may be able to help."

I had understood most of the conversation, and was overjoyed to hear that getting rid of Rada was not, after all, going to be a major bureaucratic hurdle. I interrupted.

"Arman, could you please ask this nice woman if they have a farrier at the stables?"

Although all the Cossacks had all assured me that their wonderful horses had such strong feet they would never need shoes, we had had to do so much roadwork that their hooves were wearing down fast.

"Farrier?"

I suppose it was asking a bit much to expect this town-bred idiot to know the English word.

"*Kooznitza*" I told him – it was one of the horse-related words I had taken the trouble to learn. The Customs official pricked up her ears.

"*Kooznitza? Nada kooznitza? Da, v'konyezavood yest!*" (Farrier? You need a farrier? Yes, there's one at the stables.)

With smiles and thanks we left our new friend and went to find the stables. The Director, a skinny, fair-haired man in his fifties, could not have been more helpful. He agreed to take Rada for three months at a cost of $250 a month. If I did not return to collect her after three months, they would keep her. A perfect solution!

Fed up with having to prompt Arman for everything, I decided to ask the next question myself.

"*Oo vas yest avioss?*" (Do you have any oats?)

"*Kanyeshna!*" (Of course!)

He agreed to sell us a sackful. But when the time came to pay, my proffered dollars were waved aside. "No payment is required! We wish you luck on your journey!"

Arman and I then got back in the van and drove ninety kilometres to Varonezh, a city which lies on a very wide part of the mighty Don river. I needed to telephone Andrew to let him know what was going on. I also hoped he might be able to pull some strings with his old Army friends and find a couple of soldiers to come out in a Landrover.

My relationship with Arman was disintegrating fast, and I knew I could no longer trust him to do even the simplest task. If I asked him to do something, I was being aggressive and unfeminine. If he didn't do it and I had to ask him again, I was nagging. One day I had to tell him three times that the horses needed water and ask him to find some.

On top of all that he was a lousy driver, could never be relied upon to find a camp site or even buy fresh food, and spent the entire time sulking. Worst of all, though, I had no faith in his ability to find me and the horses at the end of the day. Indeed, although he carried all my money in the van, I had taken $200 and put it in my pocket because I half expected to wake up one morning and find the men had all fled.

In short, the man Anna had provided was not up to the job. His sulking could be put down to a cultural dislike of working for a woman in a very macho country, but his incompetence was simply a matter of fact.

Unfortunately I was not able to ask Andrew for help, or even let him know that I was still alive. Although I tried for well over an hour, the international lines (or perhaps there was only one line?) were constantly engaged. I gave up in disgust and Arman drove me back to camp.

The horses had benefited from their day off, and we set off at a good pace the following day to ride to the stables. Lev, riding Rada, was ruder than ever but I didn't care. Soon he'd be in the van with the others, and I was happy with my three horses.

Life with horses can be perilous at times. We came to a river, and found Arman and Vassily waiting to take Malishka and Masha from me so we could water all the horses. I did not dismount from Pompeii. He was really hot, and decided to go into the water up to his stomach. To my absolute horror we started sinking in the mud. I shouted and turned him back towards the bank. At first it seemed he could not move, but gradually he pulled himself round and got close enough to the edge to let me jump off into the water. I scrambled onto the bank and pulled him and yelled encouragement, and after many heart-stopping seconds he managed to get himself free of the mud.

He seemed quite unmoved by this experience. I congratulated myself on choosing him.

Malishka, on the other hand, was a terrible nuisance all day, pulling back so hard she almost dragged me out of the saddle a couple of times.

We finally arrived at the stables where all the horses were to spend the night. Unfortunately the farrier had had to go to Varonezh on an urgent roofing job, so we would just have keep going until we found another one.

We took the horses into the barn. Filthy stalls, with only a few wisps of straw, but no worse than what they were used to.

I was then faced with another drama. The van had broken down.

"What's the matter with it?" I expected them to know, because Vassily was a mechanic.

"We think its something to do with the electrics."

"You think?"

The bonnet was up, my crew and a couple of passers-by were peering at the engine, scratching their heads, making pronouncements. Eventually Vassily decided we needed to buy a new generator.

"How much will that cost?" I asked in some trepidation.

"About $50."

"I wonder what will go wrong next," I said under my breath.

I slept really badly that night, and in the morning we drove back to the stables. The horses were all there, happily eating their way through a huge mound of hay each – but on the ground was a foetus. I was stunned and saddened. Whose was it?

CHAPTER 11 – CRISIS

In the end we decided it must have been Malishka who had mis-carried her foal. She was the closest mare to the poor little corpse, and she had been so reluctant to move the day before. I was saddened that she had lost her baby, and very angry with Vassily Vadianov for letting her get pregnant in the first place. Then Arman made a remark which clinched it, and made me even angrier.

"She had something hanging out the back yesterday," he informed me.

"For Heaven's sake, why didn't one of you TELL me?"

It did not occur to me at that stage that Masha might therefore also be in foal.

Malishka looked amazingly healthy after her miscarriage, but I took her out and walked and trotted her up and down. She moved willingly and freely, and did not seem to be in any pain or discomfort, so I decided to move on as planned.

Valeri, the stud's chief horseman, announced that he would accom-pany me for a little way in order to show me a short-cut. In his mid-thirties, with the inevitable Cossack moustache, he thought he was God's gift to women: his long, curly, blond hair was carefully coiffed, and from time to time he slipped his jacket off so I could admire his torso. He appeared to be oblivious to the fact that I was not remotely interested in either his hair-do or his bare chest.

He had had to be persuaded that I could actually ride: as it turned out, everyone I met gasped with astonishment to see a woman on a horse, and indeed I myself never saw a woman riding in my 2,500 mile journey!

We were riding through beautiful birch woods and across meadows, and I was thoroughly enjoying myself. Free at last of Lev and his scowls, I could just take pleasure in my three lovely horses and the en-chanting countryside. My reverie was short-lived: after a mile or so the track we were following dived under a railway line. There was a tunnel, but it was only about my height – 5'6."

I studied it carefully – could I get the horses through? Pompeii and Malishka, standing at about 15 hands each, would be all right provided they lowered their heads and didn't fool around, but Masha? She was about 16 hands, plus she happened to be the one I was riding that day so there was also the saddle to take into account. I judged she would just about fit through without being untacked. The passage was only wide enough for one horse at a time, so I handed Pompeii and Malishka to Valeri, and walked confidently into the tunnel, hoping against hope there wasn't a train on the way. Masha followed me with no trouble, and a quick glance back showed me the pommel of the saddle was about an inch below the roof. I breathed a sigh of relief as we emerged into the sunlight on the other side.

I tied the black mare to a tree and ran back to get Pompeii – I left Malishka loose and prayed she would not suddenly decided to leave us and run onto the railway tracks. I was very relieved when we were all safely on the other side.

Remounting Masha, I took Pompeii in tow again and we set off to find the van and my crew. I had heard Valeri explaining to Arman exactly where to meet us, but when we rejoined the road at the appointed place, there was no sign of the van for half an hour. Where on earth were they, I wondered? While we waited, I was obliged to respond to Valeri's questions and fend off his flirtatious remarks.

This was not a problem I would have had in England. I had just turned 48, Valeri cannot have been a day over 35, and yet he and all the other men of his age I had encountered considered it perfectly normal to flirt with women almost old enough to be their mother.

Arman and the others turned up eventually, glaring at me as usual as though their delay had been my fault. I thanked Valeri for being my guide, wished him Godspeed, and we set off again. Unfortunately I was then forced to stay on the roads – a worry, because we had still not found anyone to shoe the animals. That is not quite true: we had found a farrier a couple of days earlier, but he had been dead drunk. An inebriated farrier would be bad news under any circumstances, but it was very important to me that my horses' first experience at being shod should be done under the best possible conditions.

We stopped for a break at midday. The four of us sat on the grass, nibbling on a lump of stale cheese, and consulted the map while the horses grazed peacefully nearby. Arman's next words shocked me.

"Barbara, we have to turn south now," he said, rather defensively.

"What? Why?"

"Look at the map – we have to cross the Don, and the only bridges are one further south – see?" and he pointed to the road we were on, "and the one in Varonezh. We can't go through Varonezh with the horses, it's a big city."

"But that's crazy!" I was stunned. Scrutinising the map, I could see now that we had just been zigzagging haphazardly along. Our current position was a complete dead-end, and I could not imagine how Arman had got us there. He was supposed to have years of expedition experience.

"Look, Arman, this is a crazy situation. You and the other guys are behaving exactly as if my horses and I had rudely intruded on your private expedition. You never tell me what's happening, where we are going, or what you are doing. If you had consulted me then we could have decided on the route together, and any mistakes would have been mine as well as yours. But foolishly I allowed *you* to do all the navigating."

"But it's not my fault that the map is so bad," he shouted at me.

"Well, yes, it *is* your fault, Arman. You work for the Academy of Sciences, you were put in charge of navigating. You should have asked for a better map. Heaven knows, you haven't exactly been shy of spending my money, have you?"

Arman was silent. Vassily asked him what I had said, but he refused to translate my remarks.

By the time we made camp we had covered about fifty kilometres, but that was irrelevant since we were now going in the wrong direction. Our campsite, about a mile from the road, was well hidden behind a large wood.

One wonderful aspect of my ride was the vastness of Russia, the ready availability of campsites, and a complete absence of landowners snarling 'Get off my land'. In addition, the Russians could not afford herbicide, pesticide or any of the other revolting chemicals the western farmers spray on their land, so the ground was covered with a wonderful mix of grass, herbs and little wild flowers.

There was one other big bonus: in Russia at that time there were no fences. Yes, that's what I wrote, **no fences**. Not one. Anywhere. And nobody cared if you rode across the crops. If you were at point A and wanted to get to point B over there, you took your compass, got a bearing, and headed off in a straight line. The only obstacles a traveller might encounter were ones put there by God; rivers, bogs, forests or mountains. Not by man: fences and borders.

And I made another important discovery. Horses, like humans, differ from one part of the world to another. There is a Russian phrase for "go straight ahead" (*ydyte priatna*) but it only applies to pedestrians or drivers in the cities. Going in a straight line was, however, an alien concept to my three horses, which had been brought up running free on the vast steppes. It took me quite a while to teach them not to meander from side to side but to learn to adapt to the foreign idea of going in a straight line.

There was a terrific thunderstorm that night. We found wolf footprints around the campsite. The van got stuck in the mud. Lev found a rat in my saddle.

Oh, the joys of living rough!

Our first real test was just around the corner. Literally. Riding Masha and leading the others, I plodded along the road through pouring rain, rounded a bend, and there was the famous, fabled Don river. It was about a quarter of a mile wide at that point.

I dismounted and stared in disbelief, my heart sinking. On both banks I could see traces of a nice, solid old stone bridge which had obviously been swept away many years ago. Its temporary replacement was still there – a floating, rusty, metal horror, full of holes just the perfect size to fit an unwary hoof.

"Arman, I'll daren't even try getting the horses across that! Look at the way it is bobbing about on the water! Look at the holes!"

"There is no other bridge until you get to Varonezh."

"What about in the other direction? Oh never mind, that would mean backtracking for dozens, if not hundreds, of miles. It looks as if we have no choice but to go."

In *Tschiffely's Ride* I had read the truly terrifying account of how Tschiffely and his two horses, Mancha and Gato, had been forced to go across a narrow, swaying rope bridge, suspended hundreds of feet above a deep ravine.

If Tschiffely could do that, I reasoned, then surely I can do this!

I could not cross immediately, however, because as I turned to hand the mares to Vassily and Lev, a wedding party appeared on the opposite shore. As I watched, the groom picked up the bride and carried her across the bridge, with the wedding guests trailing along behind, looking miserable and bedraggled in the grey drizzle.

Once the coast was clear, I made up my mind to go.

"I'll take Pompeii first – he is the most sensible," I told Arman. "Lev, Vassily, please follow behind with the mares, one at a time, and *please* be careful of the holes!"

So saying, I grabbed Pompeii's lead rope and stepped confidently onto the bobbing metal planks, hoping the young stallion would not sense my trepidation. He hesitated before making the first step, but only for a second, then followed me across without batting an eyelid. My eyes were glued to the bridge, looking for every hole and making sure I kept Pompeii as far away from them as I could. I threw a glance over my shoulder, and was relieved to see the mares coming along behind us like the meek little Russian wives they were.

Once we were all safely on the opposite bank, Arman struck up conversation with three local men, of which I could only understand the gist: they were discussing the next stage of our journey. Then the little group broke up and the three natives walked up the hill and away from the river.

"Arman, what were you talking about? What have these men been saying?"

"There might be problems."

"Problems? What kind of problems?"

But Arman just threw me a filthy look, turned on his heel and walked off without responding.

Lev, however, was earning his keep for a change.

"Barbara, they say there's a farrier here!" he called.

"Oh wonderful! Where?"

"Those men have gone to fetch him."

"I hope this one isn't drunk!"

The three men reappeared with a fourth, the farrier. I liked the look of him, and anyway, I was desperate. I asked one question.

"*Skolka?*" (How much?)

All the Russians went into a huddle. I realised that nobody had any idea what the going rate was, precisely because, with no horse shoes available in the entire country, there was no going rate.

"How about $20 for each horse?" I suggested.

"*Da, da!*" They were enthusiastic. I knew it was too much when I made the offer, but my horses really needed shoeing, urgently.

So the horses were led to the "smithy," an open-sided roofed wooden structure which was just big enough to accommodate a horse. A breast bar at the front and another at the back confined the animal. Black Masha was led in first, and tied up. I watched in horror and disbelief as one of her forelegs was lifted up and firmly tied to the joist. A crowd of Russians was on hand to help the farrier: one holding Masha's head while four more milled around talking.

Poor Masha had never even had her feet picked out before I came on the scene, and behaved astonishingly well. She had a real Slav personality: she went through life convinced that this was her last day on earth and that some unspeakable horror would surely pounce before the end of the day. Until that moment, however, she would keep fatalistically plodding on towards her doom.

My dismay at seeing the foot tied up was rapidly followed by more shocks: the hooves were trimmed to fit the shoe, rather than the farrier working to shape the shoe to the foot. Worse was to come: the frog[4] was also trimmed. I had always been taught that the frog was the only part of a horse's foot that had any nerves, and therefore the only part that could feel pain. But Masha just stood there stoically.

Pompeii was next in line, and within a minute my heart started pounding in fear as he panicked and fought against the rope, nearly, Sampson-like, bringing the entire building down around his ears. But for all their coarse manners and rough speech, those Russians spoke kindly to him and soothed him, and eventually he too was the proud owner of four shod feet. And he was indeed proud. He understood that the clip-clop of metal on tarmac set him apart from the common herd.

He was a brave boy. I was delighted with the way he had walked calmly across that terrible bridge. As the trip wore on I discovered that he would follow me anywhere, as long as I got off and led him. "I totally trust you," he would say, "so long as you go first."

Malishka was last: knowing, cunning, cowardly Malishka. She made the most fuss of all, and eventually the farrier and his aides belatedly roped in the sides of the little smithy.

This episode confirmed my suspicions that some Russians are afraid of horses. Why else tie up the foot being shod? A few days earlier Malishka, who had not been given much practice in being tethered, had wrapped the rope round one of her hind feet and cut her heel. The

---

[4] A frog-shaped area underneath the horse's hoof

wound was not a bad one, but I had decided to bandage it in an attempt to keep the flies and dust out of it.

"*Nyet! Barbara – eta sleeshkum apassna!*" (it's too dangerous) the Russians had all yelled at me.

"Oh don't be so negative," I had retorted. "Of course I can do it!" I had asked Lev to hold her head, and gradually worked my hand down towards her hind leg. At first she had kicked, or tried to, but I grasped and hung onto her leg and eventually she came to understand that I was not about to pull it off. Even as I was putting the bandage on, Lev had kept up his barrage of warning advice: "Be careful! Don't get kicked! She'll hurt you! You won't succeed!"

Five hours after crossing the Don we were ready to go. Regrettably, Malishka chose that moment to come into season. Pompeii was on the job instantly. For a couple of seconds I didn't grasp what was happening. As soon as I did, I realised that I had to bow to the inevitable. There was no way a puny human could keep a randy stallion from a willing mare.

That evening the best campsite we could find had barely any grass, and while we were eating Vassily and Arman started telling me how it was getting more and more difficult to find grazing.

"The area we are moving into is poor, very poor," Arman moaned. "The people haven't got enough food for their own animals."

"And we are finding it almost impossible to find oats," Vassily said, shaking his grizzled head sadly.

"There must be oats around somewhere," I insisted.

"No, no. It will only get harder."

Vassily's attitude was so Slavic, so pessimistic, so like Masha's, I felt like grabbing him by the shoulders, shaking him, and shouting, "Well, let's DO something about it, then." Instead, I turned to Arman.

"If there's a problem, then we must overcome it," I said. "Look, your officials can be really helpful – like that Customs woman in Liski – why don't you drive to the next big town, explain our predicament to one of the bureaucrats there, and see if they can suggest anything?"

Arman sat there, shaking his head pathetically.

"Or we could buy a trailer, load it up with oats and hay."

"We don't have a trailer bar," Arman cried.

"Well, see if you can find somebody to put one on," I suggested gently, fearing he was about to burst into tears. "And why didn't you bring a roof rack, as you were supposed to?"

Again, the little Kazakh's only response was to shrug helplessly. I could have screamed with frustration. Not one of those Russians had a shred of initiative, and seemed determined to rebuff every constructive suggestion I made.

Vassily then went back to his favourite theme.

"There are many bandits around here. We're going to wake up one morning with our throats cut."

"No, Vassily, we won't. But if you're worried, why don't you, Lev and Arman take it in turns to stay awake during the night?"

"Barbara, Barbara, I need to sleep. I am an old man. Please hire a lorry, load the horses up, and drive them to Belarus."

We had had this conversation every evening since Anna and Piotr had left, and I was getting thoroughly fed up with it.

"Vassily, forget it. I've spent a year planning this trip, and paid Anna, Arman and Lev a lot of money. There is no way, NO WAY, that I am going to put my horses on a lorry – *panymayesh?"* (do you understand?)

I was exasperated by the frightened old fool, so I turned and walked a few yards away so as to be on my own. I sat on a log, lit a cigarette, and watched the lizards, toads and grasshoppers. An eagle soared effortlessly high up in the heavens.

Although there were hares aplenty, I had seen no big wildlife at all, unless you count the wolf footprints and some traces of wild boar.

I found a patch of excellent grass beside the road in a village the following day, and let the horses graze for an hour or so. Half way through, Pompeii became consumed by lust again, and mounted an ever-cooperative Malishka. The door of a neighbouring little house opened, revealing two women who obviously wanted to know what the fuss was all about. When they saw the display of rampant sex a few feet away from them, they shrieked in outrage and slammed the door shut. I giggled.

We were approaching a large town called Stari Oskol, and at lunchtime Arman and I left the others in charge of the horses while we went in search of a telephone. I was desperate to speak to Andrew and let him know what was going on, and Stari Oskol was a big enough place to have an international telephone line, or so I hoped.

As we drove up the busy main road into the town, the skyline was dominated by towering concrete blocks of flats. "Stari" means "old," but it all looked raw and new to me, and about as unattractive as a town can get. It did, however, have an international telephone line. We walked into the old Post Office's dingy interior: brown-painted walls, wooden booths, dirty beige ceiling, and a strange smell – a combination of stale sweat, garlic and vodka.

Making an international call from Russia involves a good deal more than picking up the telephone and dialling. This is how it works.

You, the customer, wait in a long queue.

When you get to the counter, you write down the town, telephone number, and how many minutes you require.

The surly girl behind the counter fills in a form, tears off the top piece (using a ruler) and gives it to you. The other piece is glued to the original piece of paper.

When the call is connected, up to an hour later, you are directed to a small, airless cubicle where you pick up the receiver and, if you are lucky, you can have a conversation with the person on the other end. The static is dreadful, so you have to speak as clearly as you can, as loudly as possible.

When the call is completed, a computer printout appears at the counter and everything gets "filed" by pushing a piece of wire through their corners.

"Hello Andrew, it's me!"

"Barbara? This is amazing! Are you OK?"

"Yes, thank you, I'm fine. Is everything all right your end? How's Katie?"

"All well, darling, no troubles here."

I told him about Rada, and about the van breaking down, and the difficulties of finding food.

"Do you think you could find a couple of soldiers to come out, un-paid, maybe as some kind of 'experience in the field' practice? I don't think the van that we have here is going to make it all the way to England."

"Oh! Well, I'll see what I can do. Mary's back from her sailing trip, by the way, so maybe she could help." Mary was a neighbour, an excellent horsewoman and very good friend.

"That would be great! But I can manage the three horses, it's a truck with a driver that I really must have."

What I did not, could not, tell Andrew about was my battle with Arman because the latter was sitting ten feet away, and it was not possible to shut the door to the little booth.

Once reunited with my horses, who had benefited from four hours' solid grazing, we set off towards the town. A mile of beautiful cross-country travel was followed by three hours on small country roads. Not easy, with no verge and coping with three rested and frisky horses.

I was very impressed with the horses: I had arrived to find them totally unfit; and then I had been forced to push them too hard for the first two or three days, but they were now well into the swing of things, and barging along as if they had spent months in training.

At supper time Arman announced that the next day I was to ride up the main road to Stari Oskol.

"Not bloody likely, Arman. We'll all be killed."

"But it is a straight line, and much the easiest way."

"For you it may be the easiest. I'm sorry, but I am NOT riding up that road leading two horses. There is no verge! We must find a way I can go across country."

"But we might lose you!" Arman wailed.

"Ah yes, that brings me to another point. I spent a good deal of money on flares, and we've hardly used any. What I suggest is that if you can't find me by, say, 7 p.m., then you send up a flare."

"Why don't you take the flares?" he wanted to know. "Then we can find you!"

"Arman, the horses would be terrified of the noise! I would have to get off, tie all three horses up somewhere, then walk for at least 200 metres before letting off the flare. And anyway, how would I carry them?"

"OK, OK." Arman sounded exasperated. "If we can't find you by 7 p.m., I'll send up a flare."

We had found several acres of oats, and overnight the horses made valiant efforts to eat every grain.

"I want to go home," Vassily announced at breakfast.

"Oh no, really? Why?"

"There are too many bandits, I am afraid. If we had more people, then we could keep watch at night."

"Well, I can't afford any more people after all the money I paid to Anna," I said firmly. "And you promised to come with us at least as far as Belarus."

"No. I want to go home."

"Arman, if Vassily goes, the Academy of Science is going to have to find another driver unless Andrew can arrange for some English help."

"I do not think that is possible," he muttered.

"Now let me tell you something." I was exasperated. "Everybody Anna found for this expedition to 'help' me has let me down. I am not going to give up. If the worst comes to the worst, I shall buy a cart and tie two horses on the back. Do you hear me, Arman? I AM NOT GIVING UP!"

I really liked the idea of a cart, which would have been extremely practical. There were, however, three problems. One was that it seemed unlikely that any of the horses had been trained to harness, and I had no idea how to go about doing this myself since I had never driven a cart. Looking back now, I am really annoyed with myself for not thinking to use the two mares as pack-horses. But hindsight is a wonderful thing!

The other hurdle was a linguistic one: I did not have enough faith in my command of the Russian language to get me through tricky situations.

Thirdly, I was a horsewoman – nothing could come to close to the sheer joy of sitting in the saddle.

At that stage I still thought I needed Arman.

An old man told us that there was a track running in the direction of Kaplina, so I resolved to take it. I had a wonderful morning, following the trail through the incredibly picturesque woods, just relaxing in the saddle and communicating with my three horses. So far from home and so tight-knit a group, the horses made up a mini-herd. If I dropped a lead-rope, the freed horse either followed on behind the others or stopped to graze.

Unfortunately I could no longer leave Malishka to run free the whole time. Since she had come into season she had revealed herself to be the most outrageous flirt, and would run over to Pompeii and lift her tail suggestively. After a couple of days, however, she was no longer in season, and when Pompeii attempted to oblige what he saw as her request, she'd lash out and kick him.

The happiness of my day was about to come to a very abrupt end. I thought I saw the van crawling along a *passadka*-lined road, not far from where I expected to meet up with the crew. When I reached the road, we trotted up it, while heedless Russian motorists sped past the animals as if they were just soulless vehicles. By the time I found a safe place to pull off the road, it was almost 7 p.m. I halted, and gazed all around looking for a flare.

Nothing.

I had been scanning the sky for half an hour before the Arman and the others drew up, all of them crying that they had been looking for me for three hours.

Again, it was my fault they had lost me.

I had been riding with three horses in plain sight across a huge expanse of open countryside. Anybody not registered blind can hardly have failed to see me.

It was becoming increasingly likely that one evening soon my back-up team would not find me, either accidentally or on purpose.

I would be alone in the middle of Russia with three horses and no money.

Something would have to be done, and quickly.

CHAPTER 12 – CRISIS SORTED

"All right, Arman, we need to talk."

After we had eaten some overcooked rice and unidentifiable tinned meat, we cleared everything away, sat round the campfire and lit our cigarettes. The lights of Stari Oskol glimmered beyond the trees surrounding our clearing, and the horses were grazing quietly in the darkness behind us. Smoke, as it always seems to do, kept us shuffling around the fire as the wind changed.

"The van got stuck in the mud and now it has broken down again. You say it is the gearbox. I do not trust this vehicle.

"You could not find me and the horses this evening.

"Lev is sulking all the time, and even Vassily, who was so kind in the early days, has now become very bad-tempered because he is afraid of bandits.

"It is possible that Andrew can get some English people out to help me. Tomorrow we must drive back to Stari Oskol and find out if there is anywhere in the area where I can keep the horses for a week or two. I shall also need an hotel, one with a telephone.

"You, Vassily and Lev can go back to Moscow. Maybe you can come back later, by yourself, to help the English. What do you think of that idea?"

The jubilant smile on his face, echoed by the others' grins once Arman had translated my little speech, said it all.

I slept well that night, having made what I knew was the right decision. Even if Andrew could not find any help, somehow I would manage alone. My back-up crew's "help" was a dangerous hindrance.

Stari Oskol contained another obliging "administrator" who found someone to help with lightning speed. Within an hour he was introducing me to Nikolai Myelnikov, a local farmer, who was prepared to keep the horses for a week or so for US$10 per day per horse.

"That is a lot of money," Arman translated into Russian for me, "but I am prepared to pay it if I am certain my precious horses are safe."

Standing in the car park behind the official building in which we had met, Nikolai and I studied each other. He was about forty, fair-haired and fat and, unusually, he sported mutton-chop whiskers. His blue eyes twinkled at me, and I liked him.

"They will be safe. I promise you." I didn't need Arman to interpret that.

"Tagda ladna!" (In that case, OK.) I agreed.

A friend of his agreed to guide me to Nikolai's house, and we trotted flat out for about twelve miles. This was like the old Cossack days, I laughed to myself! We turned into a yard to be greeted by Nikolai, some strangers, and my now-smiling crew. The horses certainly would be safe, I thought – a huge and vicious black Great Dane had to be persuaded by his master to let us through the gate, while an even bigger heavy Caucasian Arfchatka[5] was chained up by a door, barking menacingly.

I looked around: ahead of me was a fair-sized corral, while on my left was a partially-built house. On my right, facing south, was a row of what I took to be cow-sheds. A thick forest began a couple of hundred yards away, and the whole place was at least two miles from the nearest asphalt road.

This will be perfect, I thought, as I jumped off a steaming Malishka. The temperature was well into the eighties, and we had trotted hard for an hour and a half. Everyone crowded around to help me untack Malishka and lead the horses into the corral, where all three lay down and rolled ecstatically. It was the first time they had not been tethered for – well, who knows how long? They then turned their attention to the mounds of hay Nikolai had scattered about.

"Do you have any horses?" I asked him.

"Da!" he smiled, and showed me into the main cowshed. Inside were two adult heavy horses and their foal – at a few months old he was already about 14 hands. Peering around the gloomy and smelly barn I saw the horses shared their accommodation with four cows, a dozen sheep and assorted fowl: geese, chickens and Muscovy Ducks.

A plump, smiling woman with a scarf tied around her head and knotted at the nape of her neck introduced herself as Tatiana, Nikolai's wife and asked if I was hungry. I was, and said so, but was a little surprised at the offer as the half-built house had not even been topped with a roof. Tatiana indicated that I should follow her, and she walked purposefully towards the cow shed nearest the gate and opened a door.

---

[5] There are several varieties of Arfchatka – Caucasian, Turkmenian and so on. They are huge sheepdogs noted for their ferocity, and are quite capable of protecting their herds from a wolf or two.

This was the door where the Arfchatka was chained up, so I inched cautiously past the dog, through the door, and found myself in a kitchen!

It was not only a kitchen, it was also a dining room, sitting room, and a bedroom: I glimpsed a double bed in the far corner, partially screened off by a ragged curtain. I assumed that this was the Myelnikov home until the big one was completed. An archway to the left led to a completely dark, windowless area.

In this simple everything-room, which had no running water, there was a telephone, a television, and a video player complete with remote control.

Before we ate, however, Tatiana asked me if I would like to use the *Bannya*. "Oh yes, please!" was my enthusiastic response, and so Tatiana handed me a towel, took me by the hand, and led me back past the cowshed. The very end "shed" had been converted into a *Bannya*, while the earth-box lavatory stood just beyond that.

The Russian *Bannya* is a sauna – like its Scandinavian cousins in every respect, except that in Norway or Sweden I feel sure I would not have found an ante-room containing two hundred tiny chickens, barely hatched. But inside the *Bannya* itself I sweated and scrubbed and shampooed, eventually getting myself squeaky clean for the first time since I had left Moscow.

It was time to call home.

"Tatiana, may I telephone my husband?"

"*Da, da*" she nodded, picking up the receiver and dialling the operator. I had written the number down for her, including the country code. After some chatter she turned to me.

"It will cost 8,400 roubles a minute. Is that OK?"

I did some mental arithmetic – that was about US$1.80 a minute. Well, I would only be on the telephone long enough to tell Andrew I was all right, put him in the picture, and give him the telephone number so he could ring me.

"*Da, OK!*" I responded. "But why can't I just dial the number my-self?"

"This is not possible. I know this because my parents live in Germany and I cannot telephone them except through the operator."

Finally the call went through.

"Hello Andrew, it's me!"

"Oh how wonderful – what's going on? Are you OK? What happened with the crew?"

"I'm fine. The horses are safe on a farm with a very nice family. I'm going to find myself a cheap hotel room in town. When I get fixed up, I'll give you the telephone number."

"I'm trying to get a team together to come out and help you. Mary will definitely help, and I've found a soldier, an ex-SAS chap. I'm also getting hold of a truck."

"Oh fantastic – thank you SO much." Andrew had done a lot in a very short time, but that was typical of him. I was watching the clock, however, not wanting to run up a huge bill.

"Andrew, could you please ring me in a couple of days? When I get to the hotel in town, I'll ring you with that number. But it's expensive to ring you via the operator."

"What? Can't you dial directly?"

"Not according to my hostess!"

This was a puzzle to me. It seemed blindingly obvious that if Andrew could call me direct, which he proved repeatedly over the next few days that he could, I must be able to dial him. Yet both Tatiana and the operator denied that such a thing was possible, and without knowing the international code I had to dial, I could see no way of trying it.

No doubt this was just another way of keeping the Russians from communicating with the outside world – but it was very frustrating.

Nikolai and Tatiana had two sons: Vassily, just 18, heavy, hulking and very shy, hardly said a word, but 12-year-old Nikolai (Kol for short, to avoid confusion with his father) was most intrigued by the first foreigner he had met. He turned out to be the most attentive teacher, finishing my sentences when I ran out of vocabulary, and correcting all my grammatical errors.

The final family member was *Babushka* – grandmother. (The stress is on the first syllable, not the second.) She was tiny, with a soft, toothless brown face wrinkled like a sultana, brilliant blue eyes, and snow-white hair covered by the local colourful scarf.

We crowded round the little wooden table to eat. Over platefuls of boiled, fragrant chicken and potatoes somebody brought up the thorny problem of bandits. Oleg, a friend of the Myelnikov family, shook his head.

"No, there are no bandits here, but as you travel further you will find many, many bandits. It is very dangerous," he announced solemnly. He was slim and dark, and nearly all his teeth were gold. Nikolai solemnly poured us all another shot of vodka, as if it would shield us from robbers.

I fought back a smile. Not only had we been told many times before that all the bandits were a little further ahead, but it reminded me of the English Long Rider Robin Hanbury-Tenison's experiences in South America, where he was always assured that the fiercest tribes were several miles further on.

Vassily didn't laugh. He took it as confirmation of his worst fears.

To my horror I spotted a small, white worm or maggot wriggling on the table. But I was so hungry that I gulped down my entire glass of vodka and carried on eating.

"Barbara, why don't you stay with a friend of mine in Stari Oskol? It would be nicer for you, and it would only cost half what the hotels charge."

"Thank you!" I could think of nothing better than living with a Russian family. I am gregarious by nature, and I knew there was no better way of improving my command of the language than by being forced to speak and hear it all the time.

Unfortunately, we had talked for so long that we suddenly realised it was nearly midnight, far too late to go back to town and wake my new hostess. Oleg did go, however, and took all my luggage. Tatiana showed me into the windowless room, pointed out a bed, and I just fell into it. I could not see anything in the darkness, but was just grateful to be able to stretch out and sleep and not have to worry about the horses.

Here the horses and I were all safe and I could relax at last.

CHAPTER 13 – REFUGE ON A RUSSIAN FARM

When I woke up and peered around in the gloom, I could just make out that the little room I had slept in contained four beds and a couple of camp beds. It seemed that the two boys had moved onto the latter to allow the grown-ups to luxuriate in the old iron bedsteads.

Tatiana was working hard, like all Russian women. When I went into the kitchen I found her making cheese, condensed milk, cream, and chocolate butter – all ways of using up the gallons of milk her cows produced each day.

In between her dairy duties, she had also found time that morning to make a huge mound of pancakes for breakfast, which we four hungry travellers soon polished off, washing them down with cups of steaming, sweet tea. With so much surplus milk available, I was able to put some in my tea, rather to the surprise of my hosts.

"You put milk in *chai*?"

"Yes! Most English people do that!" They shook their heads.

Around mid-morning, while Tatiana was guarding the cows in a nearby pasture, my team decided to leave. Vassily hugged me and begged me to be careful. Lev and Arman embraced me reluctantly, and they all climbed hastily into the truck and sped away. I found out later that these mannerless louts had not considered it important to warn Tatiana they would not be there for lunch, nor indeed did they thank her or bid her farewell.

So there I was, all alone in the middle of Russia, with a gang of strangers, none of whom spoke English, French or German. But of course I wasn't really alone – I had my precious horses, these people would soon become friends, and my grasp of the Russian language would improve very rapidly.

Shortly before lunch, Oleg drove up in his blue Lada, ready to drive me into town. We gathered round the little table while Tatiana ladled out big bowls of *Shchi*[6] and discussed my late and totally-unlamented team.

"Arman *bl byezpalyezni*" (Arman was useless), I confided.

"*Da, Da, znayo*" (Yes, yes, I know), Nikolai nodded furiously.

---

[6] Cabbage Soup. The Russians have a saying: *Shchi da Kasha, Peesha Nasha* – "cabbage soup and grains are our food."

"And the maps were *byezpalyezni,*" I continued, "and the truck was totally *byezpalyezni.*"

Everyone laughed at first, but then the conversation took on a more sombre tone.

"We are ashamed," began Nikolai, "that your people have been so rude. They did not even say goodbye when they left! And we are horrified that your expedition was so badly planned! Listen:

Your truck was no good.

Your maps were no good.

You don't even have the right kind of horses!"

I nodded agreement, except for his last complaint.

"But I thought they knew everything about expeditions!" I cried, "while I knew nothing – nothing!"

"And so they took advantage of you. That is why we here round this table are so ashamed."

Oleg chimed in with another potential worry.

"You must have guns! In the forests of Bryansk there are many, many wolves! And in Belarus there are bears, it will be very dangerous!"

I privately reckoned that the wolves and bears would be about as evident and numerous as the bandits had been so far, but said nothing.

Oleg and I then went into town, where Oleg drove me to his shop. I was stunned to find that it sold French scents and cosmetics. Who on earth would be able to afford those? I wondered.

Oleg grabbed my arm and propelled me to the back of the shop.

"Barbara, *eta Zeena*"

Zeena rushed towards me in a cloud of expensive scent and hugged me. As a reserved Englishwoman I was taken aback by this display of affection from a complete stranger, but the 'foreigner alone in a strange country' part of me was very touched. Zeena was to be my hostess until the British team came out to help me, and I knew at once that we would get on well. She was warm, welcoming, vibrant, dark-haired, with a lot of make-up and the apparently-obligatory gold teeth, which she showed a great deal as she laughed and asked me questions. I couldn't help asking her a question in my turn.

"When is your birthday?"

"My birthday? Why, it's next week, as it happens."

"I thought so – you're a *Lev* (Leo) then, like me!"

Everybody laughed, and Zeena took my arm and ushered me out of the shop. Chattering away like the proverbial magpie, she led me to her little red car and we climbed in. Oleg, looking both resigned and amused, got behind the wheel of his truck and followed us as we darted through the traffic to Zeena's flat.

Inside we found a man and two girls waiting for us.

"Eta Nikolai, moy mooj" (This is Nikolai, my husband) Zeena said, grabbing the man's hand. *"Y eta Lyena et Svetlana, mayee dotchki"* (My daughters, Lyena and Svetlana) she announced proudly. Nikolai shook my hand and mumbled something, while the daughters looked at me nervously.

Zeena bustled around, showing me the sitting room, the kitchen, the room I was to sleep in, and the bathroom. "There is hot and cold running water all day," she announced with great pride.

I looked at her, smiling my thanks. Tatiana had told me that they were great friends, she and Zeena – but what on earth did they have in common? Tatiana lived a life of pure drudgery on the farm, although she was obviously completely content with her lifestyle, whereas Zeena and her family were comfortable in their centrally-heated modern flat. Tatiana owned one nylon dress and two pairs of slacks, and her cheerful round face had probably never felt the touch of make-up. Zeena, by contrast, had a wardrobe full of exotic clothes, masses of jewellery, and worked in a shop selling only cosmetics and other luxuries.

The members of Zeena's family were most intrigued by their visitor: I was the only foreigner they had ever met. I found it hard to understand Nikolai, who gabbled away very quickly, but the women all made the effort to slow down their speech for my benefit. This was to hold true throughout my time in Russia – women instinctively realised that I was more likely to follow what they were saying if they spoke slowly and clearly, men didn't. Indeed, most men behaved like the stereotypical Englishman is alleged to: if the stupid foreigner doesn't grasp what you say, repeat it several times with increasing volume!

"Zeena, may I use your washing machine?"

"Of course, of course. Here is soap," Zeena grinned, reaching for the packet in the cupboard by the machine. I went to fetch my dirty laundry. One pair of socks was exceptionally dirty because they had got wet and muddy when Pompeii had nearly sunk in the river, then they had gradually dried inside my brown boots during the course of the day.

"*Oojastna!*" (Dreadful!) Zeena shrieked in horror when she saw them.

Nobody who has not been on a trip like mine can imagine how absolutely filthy we Long Riders get. Out in the field we can wash ourselves every day, using a bucket or, in my case, a wonderful Russian invention called an "*oomevalnik.*" This ingenious piece of kit consists of a metal pan with a lid which can be hung from a tree. In the centre of the bottom of the pan is a hole with a bolt through it, which stops the water from running away. Pushing the bolt up with your hands allows the water to come through like a mini-shower.

So I was clean. So was my hair.

My clothes were another matter.

It is only possible to wash one's clothes when you take a day off, otherwise they'd never dry – obviously! Even then, to people like me accustomed to washing machines, scrubbing mud-encrusted garments in a bucket of tepid water is not only very hard work, it does not really have the desired effect. I had only washed away the smell of horse, human and leather, the worst of the dirt was still there.

As far as I could, I helped Zeena in the kitchen. Like most Russian women, she cooked entirely by instinct, and did not even own a pair of scales. She was busy preserving tomatoes in jars – the most successful method I have ever known. Not only do the tomatoes taste as fresh as the day they were picked, it is said that the liquid in which they are bottled is the world's greatest hangover cure. I was able to confirm the truth of this for myself a few days later.

My stay with Zeena was to last only two days.

"Barbara, we are all going to Moscow with Oleg. Do you want to come with us?"

"No, thank you. I spent nearly two months there! I'll stay here, if you don't mind."

"We'll take you back to Nikolai and Tatiana, then you can be with the horses."

"Even better, if it's not too much trouble. Um, shall I pay you now for my keep, or wait until I finally leave?"

"What are you saying? You are our guest – there is no question of payment!" Zeena was adamant.

"But it was all arranged with Oleg. Instead of staying in an expensive hotel, I would stay here and pay you!"

"*Nyet.*" (No.)

Zeena seemed really affronted. So that was that. I resolved to go shopping as soon as I could and buy the family some little treats to show my gratitude.

Oleg drove me back to the farm, where I was greeted warmly but with some surprise by Tatiana.

"We are going to Moscow," Oleg explained to her, "so we thought she could stay here for a few days?"

"Delighted!" She did look genuinely pleased.

So I settled back into the cowshed. In the end, although Zeena and the family returned from Moscow, I stayed at the farm for the rest of my time at Stari Oskol.

Although Tatiana was busy from dawn to dusk, I noticed that for her, like for other Russian women, cleaning and caring for her few possessions was not a high priority. While it is true that she herself had very little money, I believe that the Russians as a whole do not care much about anything except food. Furniture, clothes, shoes: all are cheap and tacky and totally neglected.

Now food is another matter. If a Russian household gets down to fewer than three loaves of bread, something akin to panic sets in and more must be found immediately. Virtually every town-dwelling family has a *dacha*. Although this word is usually translated as "country cottage" it is nothing of the kind. It is an allotment where the Russians grow all the vegetables they will need for the year, with a minuscule house on it, barely more than a garden shed, in which they can sleep at the weekends. And of the food grown there, not one crumb or pip is wasted, which is why Zeena had been so busy preserving tomatoes.

The people of this area were definitely superior to the folk back in Alexikovo. The men did not swear all the time, everybody said 'thank you' to the woman of the house when they left the table, and they grew flowers as well as vegetables.

My presence on the farm caused an earthquake of excitement among the people living in the vicinity, and an unremitting stream of visitors flowed through the door. I represented a unique opportunity for them to find out what life was really like in western countries.

"Do you make your own bread in England?"

"Yes, I do. Most people buy it in the shops."

"How much does flour cost?"

"About a dollar for enough for five loaves."

"Do you use yeast?"

"Yes."

"Do you preserve tomatoes like we do?"

"No – we make them into sauces and freeze them."

"Can you milk a cow?"

"No, but I can milk a goat! And hardly anybody in England knows how to do that."

"Do you know how to make a pizza?"

"Yes."

"Can you knit? Can you sew?"

"Yes."

"In England, do you have….?" This last question was completed by an amazing array of nouns: pears, mosquitoes, carrots, oak trees, wasps, apples, horse-flies, cabbages, foxes, sunflowers, wolves, potatoes, Colorado Beetles, plums, horseradish, sheep, to name but a few.

There was one very tricky question which everybody asked.

"In England, is your life better than ours?"

"It is very different, but I must say our roads are much better!"

Because of the appalling state of all Russian roads, this response invariably brought gales of laughter.

My vocabulary was improving rapidly. Thanks largely to young Kol's help I was becoming more fluent by the day, and I was working really hard on memorising Russian phrases that I knew would prove useful, such as:

"Take the right/left track by the cemetery."

"Go straight on, leaving the sweetcorn on your left."

"Keep going until you come to the sunflowers."

"There are wolves in that forest."

"Did you see the traces of wild boar?"

For some unaccountable reason, all these useful words had been omitted from my Russian language cassettes and guide-books! What I needed was a 19th Century phrasebook – like the one my father had had and which had caused us much mirth back in the 1960s. How could we have guessed then that I might one day actually need to know the Russian for "The horses have been eaten by wolves"?

"Where is Nikolai?" I asked one morning.

"Na oolitsa" (on the street), Tatiana responded, waving vaguely towards the window.

On the street? What street? The nearest tarmac road was miles away.
I rushed to my trusty dictionary. Aha! *'Na oolitsa'* also means 'outside'!

My studies were frequently interrupted to help Tatiana with cooking
or other chores.

We made the famous Siberian *pyelmyeny* – Russia's version of the
Italians' ravioli, and served with a rich and delicious garlic sauce.

We cooked condensed milk.

We picked strawberries and uprooted carrots.

We rounded up the sheep.

We milked the two dairy cows.

We went mushroom-picking.

Mushroom-picking is said to be one of the Russian people's favourite
pastime – probably because it involves free food. It is not one of mine:
endless bending over gives me dreadful backache, and I have never been
particularly fond of mushrooms anyway.

One day a friend of the family, Serioje, a nice-looking dark-haired
young man in his thirties, dropped round to visit the Myelnikovs, my
hosts. Upon discovering a foreigner there, he immediately rushed home
and returned with some *Samagon* to celebrate this unique event. *Samagon* is a home-brewed potion that is extremely alcoholic – it is also
absolutely disgusting. As I threw it down my throat, *Po-Russki* fashion, I
reflected that it was probably because of *Samagon* that this method was
invented – the effect of the alcohol kicks in before the taste does.

"Come and film our beautiful woods," suggested Serioje, looking at
my video camera.

"Oh no thank you, not now," I shrugged off the idea.

"No really, it's a beautiful day and our trees are so pretty. I'll take
you in my car."

I looked at Nikolai, who smiled at me reassuringly. Like most
women of my generation, I was brought up to be wary (although not
frightened) of strange men. But if Nikolai was unconcerned about the
situation, I felt confident that I would be safe.

How wrong I was!

We climbed into Serioje's battered old truck and he headed down a
small track into the forest.

He stopped in the middle of nowhere. The minute we got out I was in
trouble. He grabbed my arm.

"*Nyet*, Serioje!" I pulled away.

"But I've never met a foreign woman!" He lunged towards me again.

"Serioje, women are the same everywhere. And I am married!" I skipped out of his way.

Although I was apparently in real danger of being raped, in fact I had no fear at all. My lessons with Robin in London had ensured that I could disable or mutilate any man if I chose to do so; the trouble was that I did not want to do either to this poor, drunk, pathetic creature. I carried on filming, with half an eye on Serioje.

He was coming closer.

I put the lens-cap on and dropped the camera.

Hands started to tear my T-shirt off.

OK, enough is enough, I thought. I whirled round, hooked my foot behind one of his knees, and jerked him to the ground. He lay there for a moment, too shocked to speak.

"Sorry, Serioje. I'm not playing that game. Please take me back to Nikolai and Tatiana's house."

"But....."

"Please take me back – NOW!" And I got back in the truck.

With very poor grace, Serioje got behind the wheel and headed back the way we had come. After driving for a few minutes in silence, he brightened up.

"Let's go to another forest? We could have fun!"

"No, Serioje. No. No. No."

Even when we did return to the farm, he persisted in his attentions, which made me feel very awkward. Unfortunately Tatiana was nowhere to be seen, and Nikolai was clearly unaware of my predicament.

Eventually the wretched man gave up and hurtled away in a huff. I breathed a sigh of relief.

"Tatiana," I said a few hours later, "you have some very dangerous friends!"

"Why?"

I told her what had happened there in the forest.

"Oh my God! How terrible! How did you escape?"

"I learned how to fight before I came to Russia – it was not dangerous, and I was not afraid – but it was rather awkward!"

"He is usually such a quiet person, too! It must have been the *Samagon* that made him behave like that!"

We agreed to blame his behaviour on the *Samagon*. In fact, it almost certainly was the alcohol, as we later heard that Serioje had been ill for two days and had a dreadful row with his wife. When Nikolai found out what he had done, or tried to do, he was absolutely livid, and vowed never to let the man set foot on the Myelnikov farm again.

Poor Nikolai: my horses and I were creating all sorts of difficulties! In spite of a generous and non-stop supply of delicious hay, my equine companions had mischievously decided to eat the wooden rails of their corral. My kind host had been forced to create a new corral at the end of the partly-built house, using metal poles which he had to weld together – as if he were not busy enough finishing the house itself.

With my western European background, I had been disgusted to discover that the barn was never mucked out. And yet, when I went into the building there was never an overpowering smell of horse-shit or cow-pats. Sitting outside in the sun one day, watching my horses, I realised that whenever one of them produced some droppings, dozens of chickens would rush over and scuffle through the mess, reducing it to powder in the process. No doubt the same was happening in the barn!

When my horses were moved to the new nibble-proof corral, the Myelnikov heavy horses were taken out of the yard and put into the old corral. How embarrassing – Nikolai's horses had been confined to barracks to make room for my three travelling companions!

Meanwhile, Andrew was telephoning every day, updating me on my new crew's progress. We debated using Arman in some way, if only linguistically, because Norman, the ex-soldier Andrew had found, was not a Russian-speaker. The dreadful Anna had somehow got hold of my telephone number, and was issuing instructions from Moscow as to what I should or should not do. She assumed that Arman would remain on the team.

In the end, emboldened by my rapidly-improving vocabulary and fluency, I told Anna to get lost.

"No, Anna, I don't want Arman. He is useless!"

"But how will you manage without an interpreter?" she howled, obviously seeing more hundreds of dollars slipping away from her grasping fingers.

"I don't need one – I shall do it myself!" I said triumphantly, and put the telephone down.

Tatiana and I went shopping. That is to say, Nikolai drove us into town – I never met a Russian countrywoman who could drive. I had told Tatiana that Norman and Mary would be sharing the driving when they came out to meet me, and she had been astonished.

"A woman driving a car?" she exclaimed. "Can you drive, too?"

"Oh yes! I have been driving a car since I was seventeen years old."

While Nikolai negotiated the potholes, I asked Tatiana how the fall of communism had affected her life.

"You have cows, chickens, vegetables – perhaps it did not make much difference to you?"

"Not really. Under the communists, we had plenty of money, but there was nothing in the shops. Now there is everything in the shops, but we do not have any money. But it was easier in the old days."

Because there was only one thin wooden wall between my bedroom and the barn, the flies in the house had gone from being a nuisance to a torment. When I saw a can of fly-spray in the shop, I grabbed it. Tatiana saw me and laughed!

Over supper that night, Tatiana asked yet more questions.

"Are you not homesick?"

"No."

"Why not? You have a husband, a family, friends – do you not miss them?"

"No, I don't. I don't know why not – I am very much enjoying being here and sharing the life you lead. And I know that one day I will get home."

But I was no longer sure where 'home' was.

The Myelnikov table seldom had any meat on it, in spite of the sheep, chickens and the two young steers. No doubt Tatiana was keeping the animals for winter food. But this family was unusual – most Russians are obsessed with meat. Indeed, I had come to the conclusion that it was their carnivorous lifestyle that had led to so much poverty in some of the areas I had already travelled through. If they had not had so much stock, and overgrazed the land so badly, possibly they would not be so shockingly poor. After all, in most parts of the world meat is a real luxury.

More news from home: another day's delay before the British party can set out. On the one hand I was impatient to get going again – according to my original plan, I'd have been at home already, and we'd only covered about 350 miles – but on the other hand I was picking up the language with increasing speed, the horses were eating and resting and building up their strength, and I was remarkably happy on that primitive farm.

Whenever I went outside to check on the horses, or for a smoke, I took my one and only book, *The Oxford Book of Exploration*. Reading about Sven Hedin and Wilfred Thesiger was making me feel hopelessly inadequate. Then I saw a quote from Thesiger that really shocked me: talking of his crossing of the Rub'al-Khali on a camel before it was possible to do the journey by car, he wrote, "to have done the journey on a camel when I could have done it in a car would have turned the venture into a stunt."

I lit another cigarette and pondered the significance of that remark.

Did that mean that my little adventure was a stunt? Even if it were, surely it was better to do a stunt than to sit at home watching television? Whatever personal and spiritual satisfaction I might attain would surely be no less than had the wretched car never been invented?

If you take Thesiger's remark to its logical conclusion, why make bread yourself when you can buy it in shops? Why go to all the work of growing vegetables when you can cruise round the supermarket shelves, throwing into your trolley an assortment of sprayed, washed, sanitised, and wrapped carrots, lettuce and tomatoes?

Wonderful music is readily available on CD, so why learn to play an instrument?

Whole libraries are stored on computers, so why buy a real book and actually read it in paper form?

Philosophising aside, how else could I have travelled at leisure through that beautiful country, looking into people's gardens, observing the wildlife that flees from cars but not from horses, or pausing to chat to the curious locals? Had I put the horses in a lorry and driven them back to England, I would have cheated myself out of a life-changing experience, in addition to which it would have been very cruel to the animals.

It's easy for Thesiger to talk – he was lucky enough to have the chance of crossing the Empty Quarter before it was passable by car. Is he saying that nobody is ever allowed to do it on a camel now?

The following day Tatiana and I went outside to wash up the saucepans. Well, with no kitchen sink, and no running water indoors, it's obvious, really. What's more, if a pan is particularly dirty, as one was that day, you can grab a stone from the ground to scrub it out with. I sat there looking at a contented Tatiana, wondering which century my horses and I had strayed into, and almost found myself becoming sentimental about the simple, rustic way of life she led.   Why do we westerners surround ourselves with expensive luxuries?   Then I reminded myself sharply that scrubbing pans with stones in the summer sunshine was one thing, cleaning those same pans in the depths of winter was another. And, although I had enjoyed paring my life down to the bare necessities, I was not sure that a lifetime without running water or indoor sanitation would be very romantic.

"Tell me more about your life at home," Tatiana enquired smilingly one afternoon as we were making waffles.

"Well, in some ways it is much more comfortable," I admitted.   "But people are not much happier.   Nobody is really poor – almost everybody has somewhere to live and enough to eat.   Most of them have washing machines, televisions, and two or three cars for each family.   But they have become very dissatisfied – I don't know why.

"Yes, I know this – I have visited my parents in Germany, and their friends do nothing but sit and watch television all day!"

"Exactly!   And then in many ways we are much less free than you are.

"We have a million regulations that we have to obey, and England is such a small country that every tiny piece of land belongs to an individual – not the State.   This means we cannot ride or walk wherever we like, graze our animals anywhere we choose, catch fish in rivers or lakes, pick mushrooms, or cut grass for hay."

"*Pravda?*" (Really?)   Tatiana was astonished.   "But we here think your life is so good and easy!"

"Don't believe what you see on 'Santa Barbara[7]'!   No, our freedom has been almost completely eroded, which I personally feel is too high a price to pay for being so comfortable and safe."

"*Aga, panyatna.*" (Ah, I see.)   I was not sure, however, that Tatiana did understand – that she could understand.

That night as I lay in bed I mused on our conversation – I did not want a dishwasher or tumble-dryer so much that I was prepared to sacrifice the newly-discovered joy of riding along tracks or through woods.   I wasn't sure I was prepared to continue living in a country where Nanny

---

[7] An American television show, very popular in Russia at the time.

State interferes with every facet of one's daily life: wear protective headgear, put on your seat-belt, don't smoke, don't drink, butter is bad for you, do not cross the railway line, do not go out in the sun...... Yet Nanny State, while firmly rebuking us for doing anything remotely dangerous, refuses to subsidize the railways, spending gazillions on the roads instead, and encourages the over-use of pesticides instead of helping organic farmers.

I was no longer sure I wanted to go home.

But Andrew had rung to tell me that my new back-up crew had left and were driving towards Stari Oskol as fast as possible.

"They should arrive in a couple of days," he assured me excitedly.

"I'm afraid the appalling Anna is planning to meet them at the border so as to escort them here!"

"Oh God, not really? Couldn't you stop her?"

"Afraid not. I tried everything I could think of to put her off, but she is quite determined – she's bringing Nikolai Bezbatka with her."

"Who's he?"

"One of the chaps that works at the Academy of Sciences."

"Is there actually a law stating that every Russian male has to be called Nikolai?!"

"Mmm – I know what you mean! But no, there are a few other names, though not many. Vladimir, Vassily, Alexander, Oleg, Andrei, Piotr.... Oh dear, that's about all I can think of!"

"Ha! Ha! Well, let me know when Norman and Mary arrive, won't you?"

"Of course I will. And thank you again for putting all that effort into getting me some help."

"You're welcome. Just come home safe."

"Oh yes, I will. This is actually a very tame adventure – I'm more likely to be hit by a car while riding in England, or mugged in a London street, than I am to come to any harm out here!"

When my team failed to arrive when expected, Andrew started worrying dreadfully.

"What do you think can have happened?"

"Frankly," I tried to sound unconcerned, "almost anything! This is Russia, after all. But if there had been any trouble, I'm sure they would have somehow let me know. Having said that, of course they will have great trouble finding an 'inter-city' telephone. Don't worry – if Norman was in the SAS, I am sure he is not lacking in initiative!"

"And I am paying him a lot of money!" Andrew chimed in.

"Oh? Not too much, I hope?" I enquired anxiously.

Andrew named a sum that the average blue-collar worker might take home every Friday.

"That's not too bad for a week's work," I said, relieved.

"No – that's the amount I've agreed to pay per day."

"What? Have you gone mad? We can't possibly afford that sort of money!"

I was appalled. This was a colossal amount of money, especially when I remembered how much had already been thrown away on the useless Russians. And, after all, I only needed somebody who could drive the truck and help choose campsites, tether the horses etc – maybe do a bit of shopping. And of course we would be paying him seven days a week....

"Well," Andrew replied, "I wanted to be sure you were safe."

So that was it. Norman was being paid bodyguard rates, although I neither wanted nor needed a bodyguard.

"But that's far too much money," I protested.

"Don't worry, darling. And I know he'll look after you."

What could I say? Nothing. It was too late to undo the damage, and unkind to chastise Andrew for his reckless promises.

To add to all the uncertainties, Tatiana came in one day to say that the police had arrived to interrogate me. I followed her outside to find a very good-looking young man in uniform who demanded to see my passport and all the other documents.

"Where are you going?"

"To England."

"How are you travelling?"

"*Verxom*" (on horseback). Look," I pointed, "there are my horses!"

"*Pochemoo?*" (why?)

"Because your horses are so strong and so tough, and because I do not like to put horses in a lorry for such a long journey."

"But your visa is only for Moscow! And it says you are here to learn the Russian language."

"I know. I'm sorry – when I applied for the visa in London I explained that I was planning to fly to Moscow, take the train to Alexikovo and then ride back to England! Mind you," I could not resist adding, "I hope you will agree that I am learning the Russian language!"

My interrogator laughed. "But you should have registered with the local authority. You must do so immediately. And there will be a fine."

"A fine? How awful! How much?"

"And the Myelnikov family will also have to pay a fine! It will be two million." I fervently hoped he meant roubles, not dollars! Two million roubles was about US$450.

"That's terrible – it's not their fault, surely?"

"Those are the rules, sorry."

He actually did seem apologetic, but rules are rules whatever country you happen to be in. He smiled at me, shook my hand, got in his car and drove away in a swirl of dust.

I walked pensively back into the house.

"Do we both really have to pay a fine?" I asked Tatiana.

"Probably. By the way, you do know that was not a policeman, don't you?"

"Oh? Was he an impostor? He was wearing police uniform, I think!"

"Yes, I know, but I know that young man – he is KGB."

Getting on the wrong side of the KGB would not have been a clever move, so the following day Nikolai, Tatiana and I climbed into the car to go to town to register my presence with the police. The sun was beating down and the dust was swirling into the cab, almost choking us by the time we drew up in the main square.

Here I went through a typical Russian pantomime.

Before I could register with the police I had to pay 5,500 roubles (US$1.50) into a bank – any bank, apparently.

The first two banks were closed – regardless of the fact that it was a Wednesday morning.

Staff at the third bank refused, without explanation or apology, to let us into the building.

Then everything closed for lunch.

At the fourth bank we tried I was finally allowed to pay in my 5,500 roubles, after which we rushed back to the police station.

"Sorry," the desk clerk told us, "it is too late now."

I was a bit surprised, as it was only 3 p.m.

"Oh! We'll come back tomorrow then"

"No, tomorrow we are closed – come back on Friday."

"But we are leaving on Friday!" I said, hoping against hope that Norman and Mary would have arrived by then and that we would be able to set off.

"In that case, come back tomorrow at 10 a.m. It will take some time. Here is a form – you must complete it and bring it with you."

Around midnight Tatiana woke me in great excitement to tell me that my new crew had finally arrived, escorted by Anna and Nikolai Bezbatka. More asleep than awake, I rushed outside to greet them. There in the dark were the two Muscovites, looking decidedly uncomfortable. Beside them stood my friend Mary and a stranger.

Mary and I hugged each other tightly, and I looked at her affecttionately. No, she hadn't changed – shoulder-length blond hair, piercing light-blue eyes, wide smile with perfect white teeth, and a dimple on the left side of her mouth. She was 32 and beautiful.

"Oh, how wonderful to see you! How was the journey?"

"It's great to see you, too. You look amazingly well! The journey was fine, but we're a bit tired now. This is Norman," and she indicated the stranger.

I shook his hand and studied him. Norman was in his early-fifties, nearly 6 feet tall and strongly built. His dark hair was greying at the temples, giving him a rather distinguished air. He certainly looked very fit. He smiled at me.

"Well, thank you for coming to help me!" I said.

"Delighted to be of assistance," he responded.

To everyone's astonishment, Bezbatka and Anna left immediately, saying they had to return to Moscow at once. My host Nikolai told me that he was sure they were deeply ashamed, and that it was the height of bad manners not to accept so much as a cup of tea before rushing away. I shrugged, and we all went indoors.

We spent the whole of the next day repacking my kit into the Toyota, along with the equipment Norman and Mary had brought. As well as a chemical loo, which I instantly dismissed, they had two good English saddles, two well-made nylon bridles, a walkie-talkie set, and three bivvy bags. These latter were to prove a delight: they are individual Gore-Tex tents which are hardly bigger than a sleeping bag. They take but a few seconds to set up and take down, and by using one of these instead of my tent I probably saved half an hour a day for the whole of the rest of the trip!

By that evening my precious horses, my new team and I were ready to get back on the trail. At last!

CHAPTER 14 – BACK ON THE TRAIL

Pompeii, Masha and Malishka had had a good rest on the Myelnikov farm, and were more than ready to get back on the road.

I hugged Tatiana, genuinely sorry to be leaving such a kind person.

"Thank you for everything, Tatiana, it's been so kind of you to let me stay for so long. Thank you, Nikolai, and I'm really sorry my horses ate your fence!"

"You're more than welcome. We've really enjoyed having you," they chorused. "Please stay in touch and let us know if you get home safely."

"*Kanyeshna*! (Of course) What do you mean 'if'? Of course I'll get home safely!"

"*Do Svedania!*" (Goodbye) I said, turning to little Nikolai. "Thank you for helping me so much with learning Russian." Should I hug him too? You never know with boys his age – they get embarrassed so easily. Better not.

"*Do Svedania!"* he replied.

I handed over the money for my keep and the horses', and enough extra for them to pay the KGB fines, jumped onto Pompeii, took Malishka's lead-rope that Norman handed to me, and rode out of the gate. Mary was riding Masha, and it seemed odd at first for me only to have one led horse instead of the two I had been coping with for the three weeks up to our arrival.

Although the weather was still hot, the Russians were harvesting. The oats had already been cut, which meant that we would have no problems buying it along the way. The acres and acres of sunflowers we had passed earlier had vanished, and it looked as if the sweetcorn would soon disappear in its turn.

Our second night we found a good site in a hollow beside a small lake. Unfortunately our proximity to the water guaranteed plenty of mosquitoes, but our bivvy bags had insect nets, so after we had taken care of the horses and had supper, I went straight into a deep sleep.

Norman woke me soon after midnight.

"We've got a problem. The police are here."

"What?"

I peered sleepily out of my bivvy bag. Three sets of blue flashing lights blinking round the perimeter of our campsite, and two searchlights pointing straight at our truck brought me instantly to full wakefulness. I extricated myself hastily from my sleeping bag, pulled on my robe, and hurried over to a group of uniformed men standing gravely by the Toyota.

"Good evening," said one of them, a stout dark-haired man in his early thirties. His tone was distant, not hostile, but not friendly either.

"Good evening. I am so sorry, are we not allowed to camp here?" I asked. "Would you like us to move?" The policemen all relaxed.

"Oh no. That is no problem."

"Then what is the problem?" I was puzzled, and a little worried. Had the KGB decided to have us checked out?

"There is the lake!" The spokesman's blue eyes twinkled at me.

"Yes......?"

"And in the lake there are fish!"

"Aha! Now I understand – you thought we were taking the fish?"

"Now we have talked to you we know you are not fishing. Where do you come from? Where are you going?"

"We are English and we are travelling to England!"

"Wow – how wonderful! Um – excuse me – but where is England?"

"It is a small island on the other side of Germany."

"And where is your *groozavik* (lorry)?"

"We do not have a *groozavik*," I said laughing. "We are travelling *verxom* (on horseback)!"

The Russians all roared with approval, shook my hand, and apologised for having disturbed us. They walked away through the darkness, turned off their searchlights and drove away, blue lights still pulsing through the warm, velvety night air.

I was really surprised that the police should have taken such a strong line on what they had clearly assumed to be a little poaching. Apart from the fact that I had come to the conclusion that shooting and fishing wild game in Russia was a right, not a privilege, their reaction did seem a little over the top.

Shrugging my shoulders, I went back to my bivvy bag and crawled into my sleeping bag. I decided the mosquitoes must all have gone to sleep, so I left the net open and stuck my head out so I could look at the stars. As I lay there, totally content, I realised that my decision not to have a Russian with me had been an excellent one, for reasons I had not foreseen.

For a start, I knew what was going on. With Arman running the show, or trying to, I had never been told what conclusions he had reached after discussing the route, or the availability of oats, with passers-by.

Secondly, there was the question of rank.

Russians, who spend so much of their time queuing for one thing or another, absolutely love pulling rank whenever they get the opportunity, and delight in their moment of power. But because I was a foreigner, and a woman, and obviously a total lunatic, nobody could pull rank on me – not even the police.

Finally, because I was negotiating directly with officials – policemen, KGB, customs officers etc. – I was able to make the most of the fact that I was a female in a very male-dominated society. No macho man is going to put difficulties in the path of a woman who is smiling at him and appealing for help!

The following morning we had a problem: Norman had locked the keys to the truck inside the cab! The only solution was to unload the back, take the "Truckman" top off, and get into the cab via the rear window.

"Honestly, men are hopeless!" Mary muttered to me while we were grooming the horses later.

"Well, that sort of thing can happen to anyone," I replied.

"Yes, I know, but it's already happened once on the way out – you'd think he'd have learnt his lesson!" Mary was really annoyed at Norman's carelessness.

Mary and I were riding along beside a small country road the following day, Norman having driven off to try and find some fresh food, when a man walked towards us and struck up a conversation. I realised within a few seconds that he was completely insane, but too late to stop him grabbing Pompeii's bridle. Here was a problem I had not foreseen – this stranger effectively had control of my horse, and refused to let go! I was helpless. I have never carried a whip. I could have knocked him down, perhaps, but how? While I was frantically trying to decide how to handle the situation, one of the previous night's policemen came driving by and saw my predicament.

He brought his car to a shuddering halt, jumped out, walked over, and managed to persuade the babbling madman to let go of my reins.

Here was a valuable lesson: never let anybody gain control of your horse!

This lesson was reinforced a few hours later, at the very end of the day.

Three young men had managed to squeeze themselves onto one large motorbike, and the minute they spotted us they slowed down. Having encountered nothing but friendliness until that moment, I felt no fear as they approached us. Nearer and nearer they came, shouting, until they were close enough for one of them to dismount and stumble towards me. Oh my God, they were drunk!

Alarm bells clanged in my head, especially when I heard their foul language, and I called a warning over my shoulder to Mary. At that moment the inebriated biker lunged towards Pompeii's head.

Oh! At all costs I must prevent him from taking the reins, I thought, and drove Pompeii into a fast trot. Unfortunately Malishka decided that I was trying to separate her from her beloved Masha, and refused to budge.

This would be a bad time to get pulled out of the saddle, I decided, and dropped the lead rein.

Looking back, I could see the drunk lunging to grab it.

Oh no! What will I do if he gets Malishka? I felt in my pocket for my ever-present knife, prepared if necessary to go back and cut the mare free. But there was no need – Mary, fully in control of the situation, rode Masha straight at the thug a split-second before he got the rope in his grasp.

There was a cry, the man fell. Mary kept going.

At full gallop, with Malishka running free beside the other horses, we fled down the road.

I glanced back over my shoulder – the two other bikers were bending over a motionless form on the ground. Too bad if he's hurt, I thought, he deserves it.

Round the next bend we saw Norman and the Toyota. He stared at us in astonishment as we hurtled towards him, but there was no time to explain – for all we knew, the bikers were already back in the saddle and ready to pursue us.

"Just go!" I shouted.

Norman leapt into the cab, started the engine, and shot off down the road for about half a mile before turning off down a small track which led us through a wood to a clearing.

We slowed to a walk as soon as we were out of sight of the road.

"Wow – thank you Mary! I don't know what would have happened if you hadn't charged that drunken oaf!"

"It's just lucky I was behind you," she replied, smiling.

In silence we followed the tyre marks left by the Toyota.

"What happened?" Norman asked anxiously. We explained.

"Oh hell, that's the second time today something's gone badly wrong and I haven't been there."

"Norman, I never expected a bodyguard! It's much more important to me that you should be around at night – especially tonight!"

I was a little uneasy about our encounter with the drunks – although we had been as careful as possible, my horses had left a few visible hoof-prints on the track from the road. As they were undoubtedly the only horses within a radius of two or three hundred miles who had shoes on, their prints were a terrible give-away.

I was even more apprehensive when a motor-bike with a sidecar drove into our camp. But our assailants were not on board – the driver seemed pleasant enough, and I decided he was probably a local farmer.

"I am so sorry, is it all right to camp here?" I had still not quite been able to rid myself of my western attitude that all land belonged to somebody, and that we must therefore be trespassing.

"Of course! Why not?" the farmer looked puzzled at my question. "Where are you going?"

Black clouds were creeping towards us, and we had still not had dinner, so I just said that we were going to Tym, the next town on our route. I was too tired to go through the entire pantomime of explaining our far-off destination, and I was still concerned that we might get into serious trouble for hurting the biker.

It started raining just as we had finished eating. We were dry under the tarpaulin, which Norman rigged up every night between the truck and a couple of handy trees, but the soggy conditions seemed an appropriate end to a difficult and trying day. By 10 p.m. I was exhausted, and went to bed. In spite of my worries about the drunk youths, I slept well, knowing without being told that Norman was on watch.

Travelling with horses means that every minute of every day your life revolves around your equine companions. You are transformed into a nomad, seeking grass and water. Taking care of the horses' needs is your first responsibility in the morning, caring for them while you are on the move is paramount, theirs is the hunger that has to be assuaged before your own at the end of the day's ride, and you fall asleep listening to the gentle sounds of their grazing.

We had a good routine.

Norman would choose a campsite, and hammer the tethering stakes into the ground.

When Mary, the horses and I reached it, we would untack and tether the horses. After only a few days, the horses all learnt that the truck contained oats, and would hurry towards it hungrily.

Norman would unpack the truck, put up the tarpaulin, and feed the horses, while one of us would light the fire.

(While in Moscow I had bought the only feed buckets I could find – pink plastic ones. The horses neither noticed nor cared, but to this day I cannot see a pink pail without remembering my wonderful journey!)

Mary would concoct a delicious meal from the tins and sauces we carried, while I put up all the bivvy bags.

By the time we had eaten and washed up, we were all ready for bed.

In the mornings I would feed the horses if Norman had not already done so.

We would dress, have breakfast, wash up, take down the bivvy bags, put all our gear away, and finally fold up the tarpaulin. Then Mary and I would set off, leaving Norman to pack the truck and catch us up.

Pompeii was one of the most food-obsessed horses I have ever known. He would spend the entire night glaring at the camp, hoping by willpower alone to persuade one of us to go and feed him. If he saw the slightest sign of life, even at 3 a.m., he would bellow at the top of his lungs – I soon learned that if I needed a pee during the early hours, I had to make sure he could neither see nor hear me!

In spite of what must have been a rather brutal upbringing, Pompeii was also totally oriented to humans. He was happy with his mares, he had enthusiastically done his duty when the grey mare had come into season, but he did not seek their company. He was far more interested in being with me than hanging around with other equines.

Masha and Malishka were much more ladylike and had far better table manners than he did.

Big, black, pessimistic Masha, indeed, always looked slightly sur-prised when she saw one of us approach with a bucket.

"Oh? You are not going to starve me today? Really? Well, I might as well eat this, I suppose, even though I don't expect to live till nightfall."

That said, we discovered as the journey unfolded that, contrary creature that she was, the more oats we gave her, the less energy she had!

On and on we rode, day after day through the blistering heat. I tried to ensure that no horse was ridden all the time – after we stopped for a couple of hours' break at midday, we would change horses. Pompeii at one stage had a warble fly bite on his spine, which we treated as best we could with antibiotic powder, so while he was "excused duty" Mary and I rode the mares. Even then, we would swap mounts after lunch, as Mary was heavier than I.

We rode on. And on.

In the town of Svobodna, after weaving our way through the streets, over the river, and up a very steep hill, we came to a stunningly beautiful church. This blue and white building with huge gold onion domes had just been restored to celebrate its 700th birthday. This was an unusual event: most of the churches we had seen had been lying bedraggled and neglected beside the road.

In the shadow of the church Norman was arguing with a policeman.

"Oh, thank God you're here!" he hailed me with relief. "This stupid idiot seems to be insisting that we have to go right through the middle of Kursk!"

"Good afternoon!" I was clearly going to need my diplomatic skills here. Kursk was a big city, the capital of Kursk county, and I had no intention of riding anywhere near it.

"Good afternoon. You speak Russian?" the policeman responded, looking me up and down in surprise. He was exceptionally tall and well-built, with a dark moustache showing the first hint of grey hairs. He was waving a document I had not seen before.

"A little. What is the problem?"

"Your husband showed me your documents, and they say you have to go through Kursk!"

"Please show me the document."

The man handed me the piece of paper he had been holding, and I stared at the Cyrillic characters for a while, trying to work out what was written there. It seemed to be a route, but going in the wrong direction. Odd.

"Norman, what is this document? It's a new one to me!"

"It's the one which lays out our route from Belarus to Stari Oskol."

"Oh, I see, thank you." I turned back to the official.

"This is the document my two friends had when they were driving in the car from England to Stari Oskol. Now we are returning to England with the horses and we do not have to take the same route! Please understand, we are afraid of large towns with the horses, because there is so much traffic!"

And I smiled at him. I almost batted my eyelashes, but thought this might be going too far.

"*Aga! Panyatna!*" (Aha! I understand!) and he smiled conspiratorially back. "Please continue, there is no problem. *Schesleevova pootee!* (Have a good journey.)"

Riding across country the next day, we were a bit disconcerted when a rough young man came galloping up to us on his horse. Mary looked a bit scared, and I was not quite sure how aggressive he was going to be, but our fears were groundless.

"Hello!" he hailed us pleasantly.

"Hello!"

"Where are you going?"

"We are riding to England!"

And the inevitable conversation ensued about where was England, how far away was it, why did I choose Russian horses. After a few encounters of this kind, I soon became absolutely word-perfect in every phrase I could possibly need!

"Give me something," the lad demanded, "to remember you by."

"Oh! Well, I don't really have anything with me here! Wait – would you like to exchange stirrups?" My English saddle had typical English stirrup irons – good-quality stainless steel ones. They were, however, so narrow that I could only wear my jodhpur boots, and I knew that when the weather turned cold I would want to put on my hiking boots and thick socks. Russian stirrup irons, on the other hand, are crude iron, but wide enough to take any sort of boot.

"Really? Oh wonderful! Are you sure? They're much nicer than mine!"

"Yes, I'm sure. Yours are wider – and it'll give me a souvenir to take back to England, too!"

So we both dismounted, and soon the swap had taken place.

Not long afterwards, a blue Lada car overtook us at great speed, and screeched to a halt in front of us. Out jumped three men armed with Kalashnikov rifles.

My first thought was that these must be the bandits everyone had been warning me about. Strangely enough, I felt absolutely no fear at all. I ought to have been terrified, but the only emotion I felt was one of curiosity.

"Hello!" I said pleasantly.

"Hello! We are the police! Who are you? Where are your documents?"

"The horses' documents are in the truck, but it will return in a minute so we can show you then. Here is my passport."

"Where are you going?"

As soon as I told them about my itinerary they lost interest in any documents we might have.

"How wonderful! Have a good journey".

We had been travelling for a week, and it was time for the horses to have a day off. We were near Orel, and this time it was Mary and I who wanted to go shopping. I also had to try and contact Andrew.

We found a perfect campsite – a spacious green glade deep in the forest, well away from the road, and with acres of lovely grazing.

After washing all our clothes as best we could, and hanging them on the bushes to dry, Mary and I set off in the truck.

"Drive carefully, girls!" Norman admonished us. He really wanted to come with us, but of course we could not possibly leave the horses unattended.

"Do you want anything?" I asked.

"No thanks – you've got the shopping list. But I doubt you'll find much to buy. Don't forget to fill the truck up with diesel."

"OK, we'll do that as soon as we see a filling station. See you later – I should think we'll be back between 4 p.m. and 5 p.m."

Even a simple task like refuelling the truck was fraught with problems.

The first petrol station we stopped at had no diesel.

The second one had diesel, but no hose.

The third one had both diesel and hose, so according to local custom I went into the shop and paid before filling up.

As I was climbing back in afterwards, I was hailed by the fat, greasy-haired attendant.

"Oh God, <u>now</u> what?" I wondered to Mary, as I trudged back to the shop.

"You paid too much! You paid for petrol, and you took diesel. Here is some money back!" cried the cashier.

How amazingly honest the Russians can be!

With no signposts directing the way to the town centre, we had to stop and ask. Unfortunately, none of those we questioned had any idea where it was, but somehow we managed to find our way to the main Post Office.

"No, you cannot telephone England from here," the woman behind the counter snapped. "Turn left out of here, then right at the lights, and you'll find the International Telephone Exchange on your left."

We found this grandly-titled building, and I got out of the truck.

"I think I'll wait here," Mary announced.

"Really? Will you be OK?"

"Oh yes, I've got something to read."

So I went into the building alone, and booked and paid for a five-minute call to Andrew. Forty minutes later the call was announced and I rushed into on of the booths.

"Hello? Hello? Hello?"

There was complete silence.

"HELLO????? HELLO????? HELLO?"

Nothing.

I rushed back to the counter.

"There's nobody there!"

"Be patient. Wait."

That's all very well, I thought, but maybe I am paying for all this time futilely shouting down the receiver.

Back in the booth, I continued to call, "Hello? Hello?" until, after what felt like half an hour, I got an answering "Hello?"

"Is that you, Andrew?"

"Barbara??"

Even by Russian standards, the quality of the line was abysmal, and we could barely hear, let alone understand, each other.

"Are …. OK?"

"Yes, everything is fine thank you."

"..........."

"What?"

"..........."

"WHAT?"

"Where....you .?"

"Orel. The horses are well, I just wanted to tell you that. Heaven only knows when next we'll find an international telephone, but if I can't ring you, Norman will."

."......for ringing, so glad ....all right. I do worry .... dreadfully."

"No need, honestly. This is much safer than London! And of course....."

The line went dead.

"Hello? Hello?"

It was pointless – Andrew had gone. Surely I had not been talking for five minutes? I went back to the counter. The girl looked up at me, smirking. Her fantastic cheekbones were spoilt by a pinched, sullen face, far too much make-up and three inches of black roots to her peroxide hair.

"What happened? I only had about one minute."

"Nothing happened. You had five minutes."

"No I didn't. I had about four minutes before you connected me, then less than one minute talking."

"That is five minutes" the girl announced triumphantly.

It was useless to protest.

I stomped back to the truck, to find Mary fending off the unwanted attentions of an intrigued young man.

"Right," I said, "let's go shopping. What's Norman put on the list? Oh, we need food, and some decent maps. And we'd better try and find you a blanket of some kind, I know you're cold at night."

"Thank you. I'm sorry, but my sleeping bag isn't a four-seasons one."

This was a large town, so we did find some food, but the only map shop had run out of good-scale maps. Two hours later I had despaired of finding any blankets – we had not even found a shop which might sell such things. We had parked the truck in a hotel car park, so I decided on a different approach, and marched into the hotel. The receptionist looked at us enquiringly.

"Excuse me, we are English."

I had already found this to be as useful as Ali Baba's 'Open Sesame'.

"Oh, hello! What are you doing here? Are you tourists?"

"No, absolutely not tourists. We have bought some Cossack horses and are riding them to England. But we are cold at night, and we need some blankets."

"Yes?"

"We can't find a shop selling blankets – I thought maybe you might have some old ones?"

"*Nyet!*" was her knee-jerk response.

"Oh please," I begged, hating myself but feeling it was our only chance. "Just one or two, we are happy to pay for them."

The mention of money put a smile on her face.

"Wait!" she commanded. She picked up the telephone and jabbered orders into it.

Minutes later, two beautiful blankets were produced and I handed over $20. The blankets were wrapped in a sheet so we could carry them to the truck, "and then you will not have any problems." You mean, I thought unkindly, so that nobody knows you're selling off the stock and pocketing the money.

By the time we got back to camp it was 8 p.m., and Norman was worried sick.

"I've spent the last two hours working out what to do if you didn't turn up!" he said accusingly. "What would you have done if you'd had a crash? How would you have contacted me if you'd had a problem?"

"Well, I'm sorry," I replied defensively, "but we didn't dawdle. That's just how long it took. I had to wait nearly an hour for my call to England, for a start."

Although it was late and we were very tired, we still had to move the horses' tethering stakes, feed them, unload the truck, set up camp, eat…. It was getting on for midnight by the time I collapsed into my sleeping bag.

CHAPTER 15 – THE KURSK REGION

"Who are you? Where are you going? How much did you pay for your horses?"

My heart sank. Three very rough-looking men had ridden up just as we had made camp in an idyllic valley, and I was being bombarded with all the usual questions. But they seemed kind, and interested in my tale, so I answered them willingly enough.

Another question I was occasionally asked was, "Why don't you go bareback?"

Bareback? For hours at a time on skinny horses with prominent spines? No fear.

"We do not ride bareback because it is not comfortable."

Another frequent question was, "Where are your guns?"

The answer, "We don't have any," never satisfied the inquisitor. I had considered taking at least one pistol, but decided in the end that this ride was simply not dangerous enough to justify arming myself.

I can shoot reasonably well, but I do not like guns. There were never any guns around the house when I was a child, because my much-loved father would never, ever have killed an animal. So, even though my husband owned guns, I never felt comfortable about handling weapons.

On and on through that vast, unending landscape we rode, through thunderstorms, blazing sunshine, long, miserable days in pouring rain. Sometimes, looking at the map beside the camp fire in the evening, I wondered if we would ever get to England.

Mary and I had a lot of fun deciding what kind of people the horses would have been, had they been human.

"Masha would be one of those Earth-Mother types who drift around in floating, 1960s, ethnic clothes," Mary remarked.

"Oh yes! And Muffin would be the office flirt, wearing a mini-skirt and a clingy top." I laughed at the thought of Muffin eying the men whenever she went to the photocopier or the coffee-machine.

"And Pompeii would wear a Fair-Isle tank top knitted by his mother and be totally intimidated by Muffin, while secretly fancying her no end!"

And as we rode, the weather gradually grew colder and the days grew shorter.

The horses were well. About 10 pounds of oats a day each gave them plenty of energy for the small demands we were making on them. But not long after we left Orel Pompeii went lame. Tendon damage, we thought. We applied cooling gel, found somewhere to camp as quickly as we could, and gave him a day off.

We did worry about Masha, too. Although she was the biggest of all the horses, and the strongest, she seemed to run out of steam at unlikely times and inappropriate places, for no discernible reason whatsoever. And we could not give her more oats as they simply had the effect of making her more tired. But at least she never lost weight, so we just kept going, resting her whenever possible.

"Oh Norman, this is perfect!" It really was idyllic: our camp was in a beautiful birch wood giving dappled shade, high on the hill, blessed with a lovely breeze, a nearby stream, and with masses of excellent grass.

And no burrs.

Burrs and teazels were the bane of our lives for most of the ride. Wherever we found long grass, we found burrs which wound themselves into the horses' manes and tails. There were large fuzzy ones, about the size of a ping-pong ball, which had to be individually pulled out by hand. Then there were small, pea-sized burrs which dropped out naturally after a day or two. Then there were tiny ones, looking like oats, which did not attach themselves so much to the horses as to our clothing. Now I under-stood why the Cossacks had hacked Pompeii's mane and tail off: they could not be bothered, or did not have time, to pull the burrs out by hand.

Leaving Mary in charge of the horses, Norman and I set off to the nearest village, Applkovo, in search of a farrier. Our need was getting pressing, as the horses only had six shoes between them. We drove slowly along the dirt track which formed the main street, looking for someone to ask. The usual smell of horse and cow excrement was tempered by a faint scent of apples – appropriately enough, considering the name of the village![8]

"Kooznitza? Da, da – Ivan kooznitza!" (Farrier? Oh yes, Ivan is a farrier). The wizened woman I had asked gave me some simple direc-tions to Ivan's little house, where we found him with his wife in the garden, picking apples. Tall and strong, his once-blond hair had faded to

---

[8] This was pure coincidence, as the word for "apple" in Russian is *"yablaka."*

pepper-and-salt grey. When he saw us, he came down the stepladder to talk to us.

"*Kooznitza?* No, no, my father was a farrier, and I used to help him. But there are no horseshoes nowadays, so nobody knows how to put them on. I haven't done it for at least thirty years!"

"But we have shoes!" I really did need his help.

"No, I'm sorry, I'd do more harm than good."

I sighed, disappointed, but unprepared to press Ivan. Both he and his fat, cheerful wife were keen to talk, however, so we stayed and chatted for a while.

"It is sad here now," Ivan began.

"Yes," added his wife, "all the children have left the village and are living in towns."

"It is like that everywhere!" I assured them. "The young people do not want to live in the countryside."

"But they come quickly enough when they want potatoes or apples," Ivan said resentfully.

"In England they don't even do that! Potatoes and apples are cheap, and they earn good money in the towns, so they have no need to go and visit their parents."

We all shook our heads at the sorry state of the world, then said our farewells.

Pompeii's leg was much better for a while, but he went lame again the following afternoon, so we were forced to look for a campsite earlier than usual. After supper we sat round the fire discussing what to do if he continued to limp.

"Perhaps we can ring the British Embassy in Minsk and see if they can find us some stables there? Then we could send him on and he could rest and recover while we catch up," I suggested. Minsk was about two or three weeks' ride away.

Nobody could come up with a better idea, so we turned in, hoping that the stallion would be sound in the morning.

Tough little Cossack that he was, Pompeii showed no signs of lameness the following day, so, with fingers crossed, we pressed on.

As luck would have it, we had an easy day. We stopped at a village shop where Norman had bought bread, vodka and fruit juices. I asked the delightful young couple behind the counter if they knew where we could obtain some oats.

"We have some at home!" cried the pretty dark-haired girl, Nina, who was heavily pregnant. "We are living with my mother until the baby is born. We are just going back there for lunch – come with us!"

"Oh, thank you, how kind."

Although we had met some interesting people, this was the first time we had been invited into somebody's home. There is no tradition of travelling in Russia – quite the reverse – and therefore no tradition of hospitality.

Indeed, while riding across the country, we had often taken a wide, clear track ("the road" according to the locals) out of one village, only to find it dwindle to a small path, then virtually disappear for a few miles. As we drew closer to the next village, we would find a narrow path which would gradually grow into a wider trail, so that by the time we reached our destination it would once more be a broad track. We decided in the end that locals would set out for the next village, lose heart and turn back for home.[9]

In this village we spent a very happy and interesting couple of hours with that young couple and her parents in their tiny house. Sitting round a crowded table in the kitchen, warm with the smell of fresh soup, the table groaning with bread, milk, cheese, cucumbers and honey, I was plied with questions.

After I had explained where we were going, when, and why, Nina asked about bandits.

"No, we have not seen any bandits. I don't believe there are any!"

"Oh yes, there are many bandits, but not here of course. Have you seen any wolves or bears?"

"Almost," I replied, "we saw wolf footprints around our campsite one morning soon after we started. They say Bryansk has many wolves, and that Belarus is full of bears."

"I don't know about Belarus, but there are no bears in this region. Here we have lots and lots of wolves."

"Well, we'll be careful. They shouldn't be hungry at this time of year, I hope!"

---

[9] On the second day of the trip Ura and I had got lost, and stopped to ask the way. "Where is.....?," naming a nearby village, Ura had enquired of a middle-aged local woman. "Don't know – I've never heard of it," she had replied. We had found the village, hardly more than five miles away!

"Do you know what happened at Chernobyl?" Olga, the mother, had decided to change the conversation.

I was trying to eat some of the delicious food, and took advantage of every question to grab a mouthful.

"Oh yes, of course," I mumbled. "We knew at the time, and now I am making a big loop to avoid the area with the horses."

"Well, in June 1986 we went to see some friends in Kiev. We were very surprised to see that everything in the countryside was black and burned."

"You didn't know?" The nuclear explosion had happened in April.

"No, we had no idea."

I thought I must have misunderstood.

"Are you really saying that nobody told you when the disaster happened?" I was staggered. This area could not have been more than eighty miles from Chernobyl. It seemed inconceivable that the nuclear catastrophe had been kept a secret from people living here.

"Did you have any problems here?"

"Yes, a little, but it wasn't too bad on the whole."

While we were chattering away like magpies in the house, all the men of the village were inspecting the horses. We had tethered Pompeii to a tree and left the mares to wander. They were so much of a team by now that we knew they would never leave each other.

When we emerged into the sunshine I was promptly accosted by a rather drunk youth with scruffy blond hair and a moustache.

"Are these your horses?" he demanded.

"Yes, they're mine."

"That stallion is no good, and the white one is no good, but I like the black one."

"Thank you! I like her too," I assured him.

"No really, I would like to have her. You can have one of my horses instead."

"No thank you, I want to keep her."

"But I want her!" I thought for a moment he was going to cry.

"Sorry, I can't do it. Even if I wanted to exchange her for your horse, it would not be possible to take yours over the border. I have all the documents necessary for these horses, and no others."

He backed down at once: he knew all about the importance of documents.

We thanked our hosts for their kindness and wonderful food, loaded the oats into the truck, and Mary and I got back in the saddle.

We had crossed the whole Kursk region in a week.

The most amazing thing about this part of the journey was that nobody mentioned the battle of Kursk, although many of the people we met were old enough to have remembered this, the largest tank battle in history. Although I hadn't even been born, I'm ashamed to say that I knew nothing about that Second World War engagement between German and Soviet forces near Kursk during July and August 1943.

If I had known, then I would have asked the older people about it.

Could it be that the first ruined bridge I encountered (see page 70) had not been 'swept away' as I thought, but was damaged in the war?

CHAPTER 16 – BRYANSK, COUNTY OF FORESTS AND WOLVES

The minute we crossed the border into Bryansk region we left the good weather behind us. Bryansk is known as "The County of Forests and Wolves," but all we found was endless rain and bogs, ticks and mosquitoes. The rain, ticks and mosquitoes were unpleasant for us and for the horses, the bogs and swamps were potentially very dangerous, and the Toyota kept getting stuck in the muddy tracks.

Although we could get out of the rain in the evenings, thanks to the tarpaulin, there was no way of drying our soggy clothes.

I learned more about struggling into wet jodhpurs on icy mornings and digging vehicles out of bogs than I ever wanted to know. And yet, I have never been healthier, and hardly had so much a sneeze on the entire trip. I had been wrapped in cotton wool for most of my childhood, and every winter I had lost several weeks' schooling because I was languishing in bed with bronchitis, tonsillitis, a cold, or 'flu.

Mary was having a miserable time of it. After a couple of days of trudging across soggy, flat, indescribably dreary countryside, one morning she snapped.

"I can't sleep properly. I'm cold."

"What, even with the new blankets? I'm so sorry." I was sympathetic, and tried hard not to sound smug, as my own sleeping bag kept me warm as toast at night.

"They're no good. And my air mattress keeps deflating. Something has got to be done!"

Norman had had enough.

"Stop whingeing," he snapped.

Mary whirled on him like a wildcat.

"Don't be so fucking patronising! You think you know everything!"

I slunk away, leaving them going at it hammer and tongs.

What was going on? Here I was having the experience of a lifetime, while my two team members were squabbling like children in the playground.

I walked over to the horses, who were grazing contentedly at the edge of a small wood. They looked up as I approached and whickered. How philosophical they were! They obviously had no idea where we were going, or when we would arrive. Even on the first day they had never displayed any wish to return to their stable, so I liked to think they were happy to be travelling. They were a team, they had learned that they could rely upon us humans to provide food and water.

And the life they had led up to my arrival had been hard. Harsh. They had no love for their former masters, who did not have the luxury of treating their animals as pets. As Frank Kingdon-Ward remarked about the Tibetans, "...they are not unkind. Simply, they live hard lives themselves, and expect their animals to follow their example and take stoically what comes next."

Although conditions at this point of the journey were fairly uncomfortable, we were not dying of hunger, thirst, heat or cold. My spine, damaged in childhood from almost as many falls out of trees as off ponies, was happier than it had ever been, spending all day in the saddle and all night on the ground. I had never felt healthier.

Perhaps, after all, I was a true gypsy?

I shook myself out of this reverie. Gypsy or not, we had to get moving again. Although I personally was in no mad rush to get back to England, the twin spurs of winter's rapid approach and the daily cost of paying Norman meant I could not afford to dally.

I scrambled to my feet and went back to the others, who were busy ignoring each other while they packed. I had already got most of my gear ready, so I put it in a heap near the truck, grabbed a brush and went to groom the horses. They were looking amazingly well, and now they were very gradually starting to lose their summer coats.

"Oh Pompeii, look at those burrs on your forelock! Can't you be more careful?" I chided the chestnut gently. He looked at me. "Of course not, you stupid woman, I do not put my forelock into burrs, burrs jump onto my forelock!"

Masha had acquired just as many little monsters, and stood there dejectedly while I brushed them out of her shiny black mane and tail. "Why do you bother? We'll all be dead by nightfall..."

Insolent Malishka, now renamed "Muffin" because she could be so exasperatingly obstinate, was the dirtiest of the lot, and always needed the most attention. "Well, Muffin, I don't think you'll ever be white again until we get to England, but at least I've got the worst of the mud off and the burrs out." She looked at me out of the corner of her eye. "Ha! Ha! I'm going to carry on getting as dirty as I can every day!"

And so we set off again.

Riding along on Muffin in a daydream one day, I was rudely awoken by a cry of horror from Mary, who was ahead of me and, unusually, leading Pompeii. Beyond her I saw a wide, fast rushing river. Across the water lay the "bridge" – a flimsy structure of logs bobbing around on the water's surface.

I rode to the edge and dismounted. Many of the tree-trunks were rotting, and several were missing. There was no guard rail. This was worse than the crossing of the Don! But where was Norman? Looking across the water, I could see the truck with a small figure standing beside it, apparently wielding the video camera. For a moment I was annoyed, then realised that there was nothing he could have done to help.

To add to the potential for disaster, a couple of men were squatting on the side of the bridge, fishing.

"Right," I said to Mary. "If you could please take Muffin, I'll lead the way with Pompeii. The mares should follow, but for God's sake be careful! Maybe you'd better get off and walk."

"No, I think I'll stay in the saddle, especially if I'm leading Muffin."

To make matters worse, the river was about three feet lower than the top of the embankment on which I was standing, so I was going to have to ask Pompeii to step *down* onto the gently bouncing logs.

We teetered on the edge for several seconds.

"I don't want to go down there." Pompeii grumbled. "It looks very scary. See the surface moving about?"

"I know," I said as reassuringly as I could. "But you must be brave, it will be all right as long as you're careful."

"Ha! If you are so sure it will be all right, how come you are afraid?"

How is it you can never conceal your fear from an animal?

"OK, I admit it. I'm afraid. But I'm only afraid you'll do something stupid. There's no parapet, and if we don't watch where you put your feet you're in danger of stepping on a rotten log, or putting your hoof in a hole. If you promise to be sensible, I promise not to be frightened."

"Are you absolutely certain it will be safe if I am sensible?"

"Yes, yes, Pompeii. If you walk where I tell you, and don't rush, I am certain we will be safe."

"Very well then." And like an angel the brave stallion took the first steps down, then walked carefully along. The bridge was in reality just a raft which happened to extend from one bank to the other. I risked looking away for a couple of seconds to glance over my shoulder. Masha had taken a couple of steps onto the logs, but cowardly Muffin was refusing to step on the bridge.

"Let her go!" I yelled at Mary. "Don't get dragged out of the saddle, and don't let Masha stop. Muffin's sure to follow Masha!" and I turned my attention back to Pompeii's feet.

"Good boy, good boy, go carefully. No, not that side, there's a log missing there, silly boy. That's it, well done, *moy smyelly jerebyetz!*" (my brave stallion.)" Another quick look back showed me that Muffin the Fearful had consented to follow on behind her black friend, and indeed that Mary still held the lead rope.

"Be careful!" I called again. "A lot of these logs are rotting away. Try and follow in Pompeii's footsteps!"

As soon as we had passed the half-way mark and the bridge started sloping upwards, Pompeii sensed that we were over the worst. And started charging to the opposite bank.

"Hey, hey, steady now!" I admonished him. "You nearly shoved me in the river then – just don't bloody well barge off like this!"

"Sorry, sorry, but I want to hurry to safety!"

"Well, I understand but don't push me over the edge into the water, please."

A few more seconds and we were all safely on terra firma the other side, breathing collective sighs of relief.

Another obstacle overcome.

A couple of days later and we were still having problems with the truck getting stuck – its ground clearance was hopelessly inadequate for the conditions we were encountering.

One day we spent about six hours getting the truck out of quagmires of varying degrees of depth and viscosity. It seemed that every track in the vast forest had puddles two feet deep. The next morning I decided to go on ahead.

"Look, Norman, we'll go through the forest. I don't believe you can get the truck through." I saddled Pompeii and grabbed Muffin's lead rope while Mary mounted Masha. Norman was still packing the truck, but gave me the compass bearing for our next goal, a town called Klyetnya.

"I really think I'll be able to get through with the truck OK," he said, optimistically, and perhaps a trifle arrogantly.

"Well, I don't," I said bluntly, "I think you'll have to go round by road."

"We'll see. Where shall we meet? I think Klyetnya is quite a big town."

"Well, the map shows a railway line, so let's meet there!" I proposed.

"OK – by the railway it is!"

By the time we had travelled quarter of a mile through the misty forest we knew there was no way that Norman would be able to get the truck through. We were splashing through massive and deep puddles – the water was frequently above the horses' knees. But we pressed on, checking the compass from time to time, through the eerie silence.

"What's that?" Mary whispered.

"Where?"

"Over there on the left of the clearing!"

To our great delight it was a family of five wild boar. They glared at us and vanished into the undergrowth.

About two hours later we heard a dog barking, and headed in the direction of the noise. As we did so, a loose horse loomed out of the mist, coming over to inspect us. We soon found a small farmhouse, and a kindly, dumpy woman in her fifties came out to see what was going on.

"Hello! Can you tell me the way to Klyetnya please?"

"Follow this road – it's about twenty kilometres away."

"Thank you!"

The "road" was an excellent, wide sandy track which brought us into Klyetnya at midday. The first vehicle we saw was a German-registered Mercedes!

"Gdye vagzall, pajalusta?" (Where's the station, please?)

When we found the station, Norman was nowhere to be seen, but there was a large area of excellent grazing. We dismounted and waited.

Two hours later, there was still no sign of Norman.

"What do you think has happened to him?" I wondered.

"He ought to have been here by now," Mary calculated. "Even if we assume he took an hour to load the truck, another hour to get the truck bogged down and extricated, and a third hour to go round by road. It's six hours since we set off!"

"Perhaps he's injured? The Toyota could have toppled onto him while he was jacking it up to get it out of a rut. Well, we'll just have to carry on waiting,"

Then I had another thought – perhaps there was a level crossing somewhere in town, and he was waiting there.

"Excuse me, is there a level crossing anywhere in Klyetnya?" I asked a man sauntering into the station.

"*Nyet!*"

For once it wasn't raining, so our enforced wait was no hardship, and the horses were quite happy, eating and resting in the sunshine.

A group of children came up.

"Who are you?" they wanted to know.

"We are English people, riding to England."

"Where is England?" The exchange followed its predictable and now really rather boring course for a while.

But the children wanted to know more.

"Why do you speak Russian, if you are English?"

"Well, I thought people in Russia would not be able to speak English, so I learned to speak Russian! Was I right? Do you speak English?"

"No, of course we can't speak English," they chorused indignantly.

"Well then, isn't it lucky I learned your language, or we would not be able to talk to each other!"

By 4 p.m. I was seriously worried about Norman. He must have had an accident and be lying dead or dying under the Toyota, deep in the empty forest.

The police station was conveniently next to the railway station, so I walked over and marched in. The building reminded me of my school-days – everything was painted brown, and a musty smell hung in the air as though the windows had never been opened.

The duty sergeant, an overweight, grey-haired slob, was not interested in my problem.

He shook his head and muttered, "There's nothing we can do."

"But my friend might be lying dead somewhere in the forest – I am really worried. What do you suggest I do?" I persevered.

He heaved himself to his feet and waddled off through a door behind him, and after a few seconds he re-emerged with another man.

This second man, obviously a much more senior figure, led me into his office. Tall and gaunt, with dark hair and moustache, he had a kindly face and warm brown eyes.

"Sit down, please," he indicated a chair facing his desk. "My name is Dmitri. What is the problem?"

"Well, we are English and riding to England. We have a man with us, driving a truck. We left him at 8 a.m. today and rode through the forest. He could not get through because of the mud, so he went round by road. We agreed to meet in Klyetnya, but he has not arrived!"

"What do you want us to do?"

"Well, I don't know, I am just asking for your help. He may be hurt, anything might have happened. Is there anything you can suggest?" It was the only card I could play – me: helpless foreign woman, you: big strong Russian man.

It worked.

"OK, we will see what we can do. Show me your papers," and he put his hand out. I passed over my passport and Mary's.

"But your visas – they are only for Moscow," he said in horror.

"Yes, I know, and I'm sorry. I told the people in London exactly what I planned to do, and where I was going to go. You know how it is," I thought I'd try a little humour, "in London they think Moscow is everywhere!" Dmitri laughed uproariously.

"*Da! Da! Pravda!*" (Yes, yes, that's right!)

We were still laughing when the door opened to admit Norman.

"My God, you're safe, what happened?"

"I got bogged down, dug the truck out, went round, and I've been waiting at the level crossing for three hours!"

"But I asked if there was a level crossing, and was told there wasn't one!"

I had mixed emotions: I was happy to see him alive and well, annoyed that he had even attempted to drive through the bogs in the forest, and slightly put out that he hadn't driven around looking for us.

I turned to the police officer.

"Thank you so much for all your help," I smiled and stood up to leave.

"Oh you can't go now! Let me see your friend's passport," he demanded.

Norman meekly handed the document over.

"None of you has registered with us!"

"I'm sorry, but this expedition was arranged by the Academy of Sciences in Moscow, and they said it would not be necessary to register."

Norman went out to watch the horses with Mary, but I had to sit in that office for two hours while Dmitri made numerous telephone calls and instructed me to fill out some forms. The information required for these forms included our names, addresses, jobs, and salaries.

"How much do you earn?" Dmitri glanced up at me as he sucked on the end of his pencil.

"It depends – I work for myself."

"Well, how much on average?"

"About US$120."

"A month?" I thought quickly. I could not possibly tell him that $120 was what I charged for one day's work.

"No, a week."

Dmitri looked up from the form, amazed. "You earn much more than we do – I only get US$100 a month!"

"Yes, I know, but everything is much more expensive in England – especially vodka!" He laughed again.

We finally succeeded in escaping from the police station, Mary and I mounted up and we headed out of town. As we rode, I learned that Mary and Norman had had another argument while I was dealing with the paperwork.

Oh dear!

Next border: Smolensk county.

Another milestone!

On the outskirts of Semirichi we were halted by our first road block. The officials were charming, but they told us that some horses had recently been stolen.

"Show us your documents, please!" they instructed. "OK, now you must wait."

So we waited at the road block, while the horses grazed.

"How long's it going to take?" Mary wondered.

"Ages, I should think," I replied. "Let's see - they have to contact the local police headquarters here, which I think is in Klyetnya, and give the details on these horses' passports.

The police in Klyetnya will then presumably contact the police in Alexikovo.

They in turn will have to drive out to Vassily Vadianov's farm to check with him – I know for a fact he doesn't have a telephone.

Then all the information will have to be relayed back along the same route. Two hours? Three?"

Not a bad guess, as it turned out – it was two and a half hours before a smiling guard came out of his hut.

"Everything is OK!" he said. "You may go."

"May we have the passports back, please?"

"Oh, so sorry, of course. *Vot, pajalusta.*" (Here you are.)

"*Spaseeba!*" (Thank you.)

An hour later, when Norman had gone ahead to look for a camp site, we were hailed by a gang of women.

"No man!" they exclaimed in astonishment.

"*Ni nada!*" (We don't need one) I answered.

This remark was greeted first by a stunned silence, and then by roars of approval.

"Do you think," Mary asked, "that after meeting us, Russian women are going to rise up in protest against their dominant men? That in years to come people will be able to follow our route by the trail of rebellious women?"

"Ha! Ha! It's a wonderful idea. But somehow I don't think so...."

We plodded on towards the border with Belarus, through Shumiachi and Dubovnitsa.

On our last day in Russia proper, we had two interesting encounters at a bus stop.

First we met a really *sympatichnye* (kind, friendly) shepherd, who stopped and chatted to us. He was only the second country person we had seen who was wearing spectacles.

"Who are you? What are you doing?"

"We are English, riding to England." And the rest.

"How did you learn to speak Russian?" he wanted to know.

"From tapes."

"Do you have Russian lessons in England?" he was still curious.

"Well, yes, schoolchildren can learn Russian, but of course I am too old!"

He set off down the road, and as we turned away we heard the tiniest of sounds.

"Mary – what's that?"

We followed the noise, and there inside the bus shelter was a tiny puppy, soaking wet, shivering with cold, and whining pathetically. I looked around, but there was nobody to be seen except for the departing shepherd. Leaving Mary with the horses I ran after him, clutching the puppy.

"Excuse me!" I hailed. He turned back.

"We found this in the bus stop! Do you know who it belongs to?"

"Take it! If it has been left there, then whoever it did belong to doesn't want it any more. It will be happy with you kind English people."

The last thing we needed was a dog, let alone a tiny, black and tan puppy of no discernable breeding. It would be a perfect nuisance, it undoubtedly had fleas, we could never get it into England, it would need to be quarantined at vast expense. And I already knew that Norman, who would have to take it in the truck for most of the day, disliked dogs.

But we couldn't leave it there to die!

So of course we took it.

"Mary, we'll keep it until we can find a good home for it," I said firmly.

"Oh come on! You know perfectly well we'll all fall in love with it!" Mary had been a neighbour for years and knew how much love I lavished on my canine friends.

"Yes, I know, but we simply can't leave it here." However much trouble it would cause, I could never have forgiven myself had I left the wretched creature where we found her.

"What are we going to call her?" Mary wondered.

"Ashibka."

"What does that mean?"

"It means 'mistake'!"

When Norman joined us later, he glared at me.

"You certainly *have* made a mistake."

CHAPTER 17 – MSTISLAVL TO MINSK

"Stop it, Pompeii!"

It was no good, the poor horse was so cold and so wet, the only way he could get his circulation going was to prance along, giving little bucks and rearing half-heartedly. I really could not control both him and Masha from the ground – I too was frozen and soaked and had hoped to warm myself up by walking for the first hour or so. I gave up and got onto the black mare.

Our arrival in Belarus had been about as dismal as it could have been.

The border between Russia and Belarus was the river Sozh – nothing more. No barriers, no guards, just a ford through the water. The water was chest-high on the horses and too deep therefore for the truck. Norman was forced to drive the long way round, while Mary, the horses and I waited on the Belarus side with our backs to driving, icy rain for an hour.

By the time Norman reached us, it was almost dark, so we had no choice but to make camp on the exposed hillside where we had met up.

Oh how I blessed my sleeping bag that night! We were soaked, frozen and exhausted when we went to bed, but I soon warmed up once I'd got my clothes off and crawled into my cosy cocoon. Tiny as she was, Ashibka helped, too, as she snuggled up to my side. To my great relief her fleas were too snobbish to want to leave a good, woolly Russian dog and pester a foreign human.

The next morning was a different matter.

It took an iron will to get out of the sleeping bag.

It took all my courage – and strength – to pull on my sodden jodhpurs.

And I still had to emerge from the bivvy bag!

Swearing and struggling, we tacked up the soaked horses, packed our gear as quickly as possible, and set off for the nearest town, Mstislavl. Head down against the driving rain, cocooned in soggy misery, I almost missed an important clue. The horse pulling a cart in the opposite direction had hooves which clip-clopped! Starting from my reverie, I dashed over to interrogate him.

"Good morning! Where did you get those horseshoes?"

"At the *Konyezavod!*" *Konyezavod?* Was that a village?

"And is there a farrier at the *Konyezavod?*"

"Da, da, yest." (Yes, there is.)

"Bolshoi spaseeba," I thanked him, and hurried to catch up with Mary.

"What was all that about?" she asked.

"Didn't you hear his horse? It had shoes on! He says there's a farrier at *Konyezavod*!"

"Where's that?"

That was a good question, but we were very close to the centre of town, so I decided to wait and make enquiries there. As I rode, something kept nagging at my frozen brain. Of course! *Konyezavod* translates literally as "horse factory" – there must be a stud somewhere!

Mstislavl was a pretty town full of shops, and the houses were surrounded by neat and tidy gardens. This was very obviously a different country.

Near the centre of town we found Norman talking to a crowd of policemen, all very welcoming and friendly. I interpreted – Norman wanted to change some money, but had been having difficulties because it was a Saturday.

As my Belarus visa was already hopelessly out of date, and as I did not relish the thought of spending time in gaol there, I asked the kind policemen what I should do.

"Nye znayo!" (Don't know) they chorused cheerfully.

As we stood there chatting, shivering in the continuing downpour, our new friends asked why we did not check into a hotel.

"Does the hotel also take horses?" I asked, without any hope of a positive response. The thought of a dry, warm room and running water was dangerously seductive.

But the horses were even more soggy and unhappy than we were.

"No, but there are excellent stables at *Konyezavod*! They breed Ardennes horses there."

"Oh how fantastic! Where is it, please?"

It was only about four miles: I translated the directions for Norman, swung back in the saddle, and we headed out of town.

After getting lost once, we finally made it to the stables, where we were greeted by the very kind director, Oleg.

"Hello! Excuse me, but we are English and riding to England. Can we leave our horses here until Monday?"

"Of course!!"

"And, do you have a farrier?"

"Yes, yes. But we have no shoes!"

"That doesn't matter – I have my own shoes."

"Good. We will arrange it."

We climbed into the truck and Norman drove to the hotel. This would mark the first time we had not camped out since we left the Myelnikov farm in faraway Stari Oskol, so I looked forward to clean sheets and a hot bath.

But it was not to be.

We may have been in Belarus, but Russian rules still applied. We booked two rooms, and Mary and I walked into ours with great anticipation. We had two beds, and an adjoining bathroom. Sounds good? Yet again I was reminded of school: brown paint and stale smells. The beds were lumpy, the bathroom had an ancient, filthy loo, and the hot tap did not work.

On the plus side, we were out of the rain and could, at long last, dry our riding clothes. And the cold tap in the bathroom did work – running water at last!

It was time for lunch, so we went into the hotel restaurant. Well, out there it was a restaurant, but in any Western country it would have more truthfully been described as a canteen. The walls and ceiling were an institutional pale green, the tables were square, Formica-covered and very wobbly. The other tables were all occupied by young men in varying degrees of sobriety.

"*Vot menu,*" the waitress handed us the menu. It was valid from 15th to 17th September (today it was 16th), and listed at least fifty dishes. Wow! Our waitress ticked three of them.

"Are those three meals not available?"

Her face said quite clearly "You stupid foreign woman!" but her mouth replied, "No, these are the ones which *are* available."

"Ah, of course. How silly of me!"

While she went to get our order, Mary, Norman and I discussed this:

"But why put so many items on the menu when you know you're not going to be able to provide them?" Mary wondered.

"Perhaps the cook thinks of all the dishes she would like to be able to produce, if she could get the ingredients, and puts them on the menu. Then she goes shopping and makes do with whatever is available," I suggested. "Oh look! They've actually got wine on the menu - shall we have some? I haven't had any since Moscow!"

"Mmm, that would be great!" Mary agreed enthusiastically.

"What have they got?" Norman squinted at the Cyrillic characters.

"Er... let me see, apart from the Georgian wine I love so much I know absolutely nothing about the wines they have here. Let's ask."

When the waitress returned, I said, "What kind of wine do you have?"

"Come with me and you can choose," she answered.

When I followed her to the serving area at the back I found one solitary bottle. It was Hungarian, and I thanked the waitress and said, "OK, we'll have this one," and walked back to the others.

A few minutes later she brought the bottle. She also brought the corkscrew and handed it to Norman with a look of defiance on her face: she had absolutely no idea how to use it but was not going to admit it. Norman looked at the bottle, at the waitress, and at me.

"Oh Norman, don't tease her!" I kept a straight face, and turned to the poor girl who was trying to look as though the situation had not got out of hand.

"Thank you for bringing the wine. Is it all right if we open the bottle ourselves?"

"Of course!"

After lunch I decided that, as Chernobyl was getting rapidly closer, it really was time to buckle down and translate the instructions for the Geiger-counter. This was a very time-consuming and incredibly frustrating chore, as of course I had to look up almost every word in the dictionary, and the result was still completely unintelligible. What the hell, I decided in the end, I'll give it to a native to read and ask him which bits are important and to explain them to me in simple language.

Although the food and wine had gone some way towards taking the chill off our bodies, I thought a visit to the *Bannya* would get us thoroughly clean as well as warm. We knew where it was, as we had passed it while riding into town, so, grabbing a change of clothes, we jumped into the truck and drove the half mile there. The building was huge, with massive stone walls and an indefinable similarity to a public swimming bath. We paid a few roubles at the wood-panelled entrance, in exchange for which we were handed a moth-eaten towel each and directed through an open doorway which led to a wide corridor with two closed doors on each side.

"Now what?" asked Mary.

I looked at the initials on the doors – in that part of the world the words for "Ladies" and "Gentlemen" were usually shortened to the initial letters. One door had "Ж" on it – short for "jenshina," "woman," so I boldly opened it and we walked through.

The similarities with a public swimming pool continued: the room we entered was wide, high-ceilinged, and lined with white tiles, and we saw basins and showers along one wall. In one corner there was a thick door with a glass panel – the *Bannya* itself. Stripping off our clothes, we wrapped the little towels around us, entered the enveloping, moist warmth of the sauna and lay down gratefully. Oh, what utter, utter bliss!

"Who are you?" The question was sharp and the tone of voice decidedly frosty. I opened my eyes to see a large, dark-haired woman in her thirties glaring down at me.

"Hello!" I smiled. Anywhere on the planet, polite friendliness can almost always transform confrontation into dialogue. "We are English. My name is Barbara and this is Mary."

"English?? How amazing! My name is Lyuba," and with these reassuring words, our new friend rushed out of the *Bannya,* stripped off her own clothes, and returned to beat us with the regulation birch twigs.

"Why are you here? What are you doing? Where are you going?"

So we sat there sweating, our skins glowing pink as much from the beating as from the intense heat, while I told Lyuba all about our journey. She made the most wonderful audience, oo-ing and ah-ing in all the right places, clearly thrilled to hear my tale.

Eventually we left, with some reluctance, the tiny, hot room and stood under hot showers for a few minutes, before dressing again in some clean clothes.

"Guess what?" she told everybody within hearing. "These people are English! They are here with horses – they have ridden here all the way from Volgograd! And they are going to England."

An assortment of plump, naked women looked suitably impressed. I realised that I had reached a watershed: for the first few weeks of my journey, people had been amazed to hear about my far-off destination, but here for the first time they were even more astonished by how far my horses and I had already travelled.

"Now you must have water," Lyuba insisted, handing us each a cup of tooth-achingly sweet fruit juice, quickly snatched away and replaced by a little glass of vodka and a biscuit.

At our suggestion, Lyuba joined us for supper that night, but she was a Slav: so within an hour she was hopelessly drunk, unshakeably melancholic, and wept inconsolably until we managed to load her into the truck and drive her home.

Why are the Slav people so melancholy? Why do most of the famous Russian books, short stories, even folk songs, have unhappy endings?

"It is because we have always been oppressed," was the solution put forward by most westernised Muscovites.

"Well, I know you've been oppressed for centuries," I countered, "but then so have a lot of people, the Africans for example. And look at them! Happy rhythms, wonderful music, much laughter!"

"But not like us!" the Russians claimed.

My theory is that the Slav people have become sad and pessimistic because of the long, long, dark cold winters. Whatever the explanation, I found over and over again that if you give a Slav two or three vodkas, you can guarantee floods of tears and a genuinely deep unhappiness.

We were back at the *Konyezavod* two days later, the horses having benefited from their rest and endless supply of tasty hay and local oats. For myself, having luxuriated in heated rooms, washed and dried my clothes and got really clean myself, I was ready to move on.

But we had to wait two hours for the farrier.

As soon as he saw the horses, he came over to me.

"That white horse is in foal! You must keep her under cover!"

How did he know?

"Yes, we thought she might be in foal. But we are riding to England, it is not possible to find a stable every night!"

He shrugged.

While he worked the stable lads clustered around to grumble about their poverty.

"We work so hard, but all we can buy with our wages is bread and cigarettes!" I knew this to be true. I also knew that they grew all their own food and seldom went hungry. Putting shoes on their children's feet was another matter.

"Your life must be quite different," they said enviously, "in the West you are all very rich!"

"Ah no!"   I was determined to do everything in my power to straighten this misconception.   "Life is very different, it is true, and we do have more money than you do.   But we have to work very hard.   One person does as much work as three or four people here.   And thousands and thousands of people do not have jobs at all!"

"But you are paid more?"

"Of course we are paid more!   But everything is much more expensive.   For example, in England a bottle of vodka costs $15."

"Really?"   Eyebrows shot up.   "It's only $1 here."

"I know.   And we have to pay at least $750 for a new saddle!"

"$750?   Are you serious?   We can buy a new car for that!"

"Exactly."

Finally we got tacked up and back on the road.   The delightful director of the stud refused to take any payment, for which we were extremely grateful and somewhat embarrassed.

The locals were harvesting the linseed crop.   As we rode through the flat landscape, I watched as dozens, scores of people laboured all around and I felt as though I had become part of a Breughel painting.   When we stopped to camp on the edge of one of these areas, I saw to my astonishment that each individual stook (sheaf of about a hundred linseed stalks) was bound by hand.   A gross or two of these stooks went into a stack, and hundreds of stacks stood in rows as far as the eye could see.

The linen stalks were forked generously onto lorries.   These overloaded vehicles, looking like a cross between a thatched cottage and a hedgehog, frightened Pompeii almost to insanity as they hurtled down the roads at 60 mph or so heading, as we were to discover later, for Minsk and the linen factories.

The most dangerous episode of that stretch came when we reached Shlof – a large town, but unavoidable because it had the only bridge across the river.

Ah rivers!   By this stage I only had to see a blue line on the map to shy back like a startled horse.   Experience had taught me that bridges were either terrifyingly insubstantial, if not downright life-threatening, or they were solid concrete structures with a volume of traffic that would not have disgraced a motorway.

I really thought Pompeii and I were going to meet our Maker as we crossed Shlof bridge.   Norman was driving the truck behind, so as to protect our rear, but we had no control over the traffic coming towards us, and Pompeii shied and skittered at every oncoming lorry. By the time we got to the centre of the bridge, I was seriously concerned that the stallion was going to leap the low parapet. Would I get my feet out of the stirrups before we hit the water? I believe I would have, but thank God I did not have to find out – Pompeii and I made it safely to the other side.

Shaken and frightened, I decided that from then on I would get off and lead the horse, especially as he was always so trusting and docile when I was beside, rather than on top of, him.

Our other constant nagging worry was on behalf of the horses' welfare. They had lost weight in the five days since the terrible night of our crossing into Belarus, and Pompeii's girth was two holes tighter. I knew that once they grew their winter coats they would be all right, but it was only mid-September, and a mere six weeks earlier we had all been roasted by the blazing sun. And as the nights grew longer and colder, the grass would become even less nutritious.

The horses were getting just over a bucket of oats a day each, plus the vitamin powder I had brought from England, and we were stopping twice a day to graze them, but I was concerned about what lay ahead. When Norman and Mary had set out from England, I had asked Andrew to put ten bales of Horsehage[10] into the truck, as I had foreseen this problem. Unfortunately the team had only brought three bales. I had said nothing at the time, but it had irritated me that they had brought a chemical loo, an absurdity which must have taken up at least as much room as two bales of Horsehage, a necessity.

But I had to make do with what I had, not what I wished for. Until the horses grew their winter coats, they'd have to be given more oats and we would have to find the most sheltered places we could find to camp.

And so we plodded on, day after day, across the flat, late autumn landscape. It was usually either bitterly cold, or it rained, but never as much as in Bryansk, for which I was extremely thankful. On the rare occasions the weather brightened up, flies and mosquitoes would materialise to torment us.

The good news was that we found a home for little Ashibka! We gave her to an old man who had come up to chat to us when we were having lunch beside the road one day.

---

[10] Wilted hay in airtight plastic sacks – clean , compact, and dust-free.

I hated saying goodbye to the dear little puppy, but I knew we could not keep her, and her new owner seemed very kind. At least she was better off than she would have been if we had left her at the bus shelter.

Norman and Mary studiously avoided one another as far as possible, then bickered away when some kind of interaction was necessary.

In spite of my worry about the horses, the miserable weather, and the warfare between the other members of my team, I was extremely happy.

We were approaching Minsk, the capital of Belarus. The British Ambassador there had kindly recommended some stables, grandly named "Olympic Stables," near the city.

"I hope you're not going to ride through Minsk?" he had enquired anxiously when I spoke to him on the telephone. "I don't think it's allowed!"

"Oh no," I had laughingly reassured him. "We avoid big towns wherever possible. But thank you so much for your advice."

One evening we were studying the map, and Norman and I were discussing whether it was better to go north round Minsk, or south. Either way, it would add a day's ride. While I would have been perfectly happy to spend the rest of my life on this journey, Mary was in a hurry to get to Poland, where she would leave the team. Plus, always in the back of my mind was the fact that Norman was being paid by the day.

I forgot my conversation with the Ambassador.

"Look, it's Sunday in a couple of days – why don't we just ride right through the middle of Minsk? There won't be much traffic, and it'll save us a day."

"Oh yes, that's a great idea!" Norman and Mary were both enthusiastic.

And so it was agreed. We would ride up the dual carriageway right into Minsk, and on out the other side to the stables we had been recommended.

CHAPTER 18 – MINSK TO GRODNO

Instead of trotting for ten minutes, walking for ten minutes, which was the system we had been using, we tried just having a lot of short trots. In this way we broke the 40 mile (sixty-five) kilometre barrier for the first time, and arrived within about fifteen miles of Minsk. We found a wonderfully sheltered clearing deep in a conifer wood and started to make camp. We went about our usual evening chores, almost on auto-pilot, with no premonition that disaster was about to strike.

Mary was starting to prepare our meal while I put up the bivvy bags and Norman shovelled oats into buckets. As usual, I stopped what I was doing to walk over and help him feed the horses. As I approached her with her feed, Masha, the least greedy and most sensible of all the horses, got tangled up in her tether, panicked, and fell over on the rather uneven ground. To my absolute horror, instead of heaving herself back onto her feet, she just lay there motionless.

"Oh my God, what's she done?" I cried as I rushed over to the supine body.

Norman had fed Pompeii and Muffin and ran over to help.

Masha just lay there, looking tiny as all horses do when they lie down. She was breathing, and looked up at me pathetically. Mary appeared at my side.

"We've got to get her up," said Norman calmly.

Suiting the action to the word, he grabbed her rope and tugged. Mary and I went round to the mare's other side and encouraged her to her feet with a combination of clicks, cries and cajoling.

Getting her up was one thing, keeping her on her feet was another – every time we let go, she started to crumple again.

"What's happened to her neck?" I asked, anguished. "Do you think it's broken?" Masha was holding her head at a most peculiar angle.

"She must have done something to it when she fell," Norman said, stating the obvious.

Masha was persuaded to walk a few steps. No problems there, she was mobile, in spite of the strange way she held her head. And, although she was sweating, she didn't seem to be in any pain.

We let her go, and she started to fall again.

What, I wondered, do you do with a horse that can't stand up? How far was the nearest vet? How would we manage the following day? I had some bute (a very effective painkiller for horses), so if it looked as though she was hurting, we could at least drug her up enough to get her to the stables on the other side of Minsk.

We took it in turns to walk her up and down, up and down. After about two hours the big black mare was moving much more freely and, more significantly, could stand up unaided.

"Well, we'll have to leave her loose," I said. "There's no way I'm going to tether her tonight. She's the most likely to wander off, but I doubt if she'll go very far with Pompeii and Muffin here."

"Oh, absolutely," said Mary.

We ate our supper in shifts as we walked Masha around, and Norman announced that he would check her at hourly intervals during the night, so Mary and I could get some sleep before our long day's ride.

I crawled into bed after a last check on poor Masha, but slept very badly. We were so vulnerable, I thought at first. Could we get help? Would the vet, if we could find one, be skilled enough and have the right kind of drugs available? I worried myself sick for about half an hour before pulling myself together.

We were in Belarus, not on the moon.

Minsk was less than half an hour's drive away, and we had a truck.

Soviet vets were superbly trained, and I was sure the right kind of drugs, if they proved necessary, could be found – for a price.

Norman woke us up at 4.45 a.m. with the most welcome news that Masha had just got down, rolled, and got up again.

"I checked her several times in the night," he told me, "and so did Mary."

"Oh wonderful, thank you so much. I really am grateful."

"Well, actually we had to walk miles to find her – she had wandered off deep into the forest!"

I dressed hastily and walked over to inspect the mare.

As usual, she had left half her oats and was nibbling disconsolately on a tuft of grass. At my approach she lifted her head and looked at me.

"Masha, are you all right now?" I looked at her carefully. She was holding her head at a perfectly normal angle and was obviously not in any pain. "Will you be able to get to the other side of Minsk?" I walked her for a hundred yards or so, and could see absolutely nothing wrong with her at all.

"I think she must have cricked her neck when she fell," I said to the others. "I've never known a horse do it, but when I do it it's agony for a few seconds, then the neck is stiff for a few hours, after which I'm fine."

"Yes," agreed Mary. "She certainly looks 100% OK this morning!"

So with very few misgivings I saddled and mounted Pompeii, grabbed Masha's lead-rope, and we set off at 6.30. It was too dark to see our way through the thick fir trees, so Norman followed us with headlights blazing. As soon as we emerged from the forest, however, we could see quite well.

The weather was perfect for riding – cool and cloudy, and therefore fly-free. Masha was moving so freely that we even risked a couple of canters, and covered about thirteen miles or so by lunchtime.

Unfortunately we were obliged to ride along the "motorway" – a dual carriageway with no central reservation – but the verges were wide and Pompeii was on his best behaviour for a change.

When we arrived in Minsk we found it very crowded with people, but not with big lorries. And it was a town that could have been designed with horses in mind: parallel with the main road was a smaller, service road, so what traffic there was caused us no problem.

"Who are you? Where are you going?" some tipsy young men called out.

They didn't believe my answer, and started throwing empty cans at us.

"To hell with this, Mary, let's get a move on," I called, and we trotted out of range.

We stopped about half-way through to give the horses a short break and let them graze on a welcome patch of grass.

"Look!" Mary pointed at the building behind us. "A casino!"

So it was: a neon picture of a pack of cards and a martini glass reminded us most forcefully that we were now in "civilisation."

Or almost. Within half a mile of the city centre we found tethered cows grazing peacefully between the obligatory Stalinist Soviet-style blocks of flats.

"How much further do we have to go, Norman?" There had been no opportunity all day to empty my bladder, and I was keen to get out of the city, off the main roads, and find a bush.

Norman consulted the map.

"It's about another eight kilometres to the turn off, according to this."

"Five miles? Oh, that's all right, I can manage for another hour or so!"

We found the stables the Embassy had recommended. They may have been called "Olympic Stables" but there was nothing remotely Olympian about them – they consisted of a couple of stable blocks, a series of scruffy huts and an extremely primitive hotel.

As usual, however, the people there were very kind and we led our horses into some very small and dark loose-boxes at the back, and asked that they be given limitless quantities of hay and oats.

"I've booked us into the hotel," Norman announced. But when we asked about food, hot water, and telephones, the answer was a big fat zero: *"Nyet"* to all three.

"Oh this is ridiculous! If we're so close to Minsk, we need to ring Andrew and I for one want a hot bath and a hot meal," I insisted. "Let's go back into town – we have to go there anyway to make a telephone call, so we might as well find a decent hotel while we're at it!"

"Hear, hear!" chimed in Mary.

Norman looked really put out, and when we approached the truck I realised why – he had unpacked it while we were seeing to the horses.

"I'm going to stay here whatever happens," he said sulkily.

"Fine," I said lightly, not wanting any more arguments. "But let's drive back and see if we can find a reasonable hotel."

We squished into the cab of the truck and headed back the way we had come, in search of a good meal and a comfortable room.

"Er, how do we find a hotel?" Mary wanted to know.

"Well, we must look for the Russian word for hotel, "Гостиница" I replied optimistically. But such hotels as there may have been were remarkably modest about their charms, and we could not find even one.

"We can't drive around all night," Norman pointed out irritably.

"No, you're right. What are we going to do?"

"I know," said Mary, her face brightening, "we can go back to the casino! They are sure to be able to help us."

"Oh brilliant! Well done – let's do that."

In a few minutes' time we drew up beneath the glowing pink martini glass.

"You girls hop out and see what you can do while I park the truck," said Norman.

So we climbed out of the cab and walked boldly in through the front door of the casino.

Inside a palatial high-ceilinged entrance hall, lined with vivid blue marble tiles, a man and two women looked at us in disdainful silence.

They were dressed entirely appropriately for a casino or cocktail bar. We were not.

We were dressed in grubby jodhpurs, coats, scarves and hats.

I had nothing to lose.

"Good evening! We're English, and I wonder if you could help us?"

"English? Really?" the man, tall and well-built – rather too well-built for his dinner jacket – had switched on a radiant smile. The girls thawed, too.

"What can we do for you?" asked the blond one wearing a very short dress in an improbable shade of green.

"We need food, and then we need to find a good hotel – one from which I can telephone England."

"*Prekrasna!*" (Wonderful!) cried the other girl, a brunette who was wearing lurid pink and enough make-up to sink a battleship. And she clapped her hands in genuine pleasure.

The man, still smiling beneath his dark moustache, made a decision.

"You must eat here. While you eat we will book you into a good hotel."

Norman had walked in and was standing beside us. Neither he nor Mary needed any translation: the smiles said everything that needed to be said.

"*Nyet! Ni vasmojne!*" I was aghast. We could not possibly sit down at table in a smart restaurant dressed as we were.

"*Da! Da!*"

"But look at our clothes! We have been riding horses from Volgograd and we have been camping nearly all the way! We can't possibly sit in your beautiful dining room."

"It doesn't matter," the man insisted. "We give you good food and nice drinks while we find you a hotel."

We vanished into the cloakrooms and did our best to tidy up, but without much success. I defy anyone to transform jodhpurs and a woolly pullover into anything acceptable in a smart restaurant. But we washed our faces and hands, and brushed our hair, and returned to the lobby feeling very embarrassed and distinctly underdressed.

"Come! Follow me!" cried the blond and teetered on her stiletto heels up a sweeping staircase to the first floor. The three of us followed, cringing at the thought of making a grand entrance into the restaurant, which no doubt would be full of overdressed "new Russians" – or rather, "new Belarussians."

At the top of the stairs we came face to face with a magnificent set of intricately carved double doors.   Our hostess flung them open dramatically and urged us into the room beyond.

It was empty!

We were the only customers!

We sat down, mightily relieved, and the two glamorous girls became our waitresses.

"Would you like something to drink?"

"Yes please. Norman? Mary?"

"Gin and tonic, please," they chorused. I chose wine.

"How much gin would your friends like? How much tonic?"

Russians don't have "measures" as the British do, but they do dispense alcohol in units of centilitres. "Will you have 50 centilitres?" is a common question, even in a private house. As for the tonic, Russians never put mixers in with their drinks, and therefore had no idea what sort of proportions to offer. I held up a glass and pantomimed an acceptable level of gin, and asked for it to be topped up with tonic.

"What kind of music would you like?"

"Oh – do you have Russian folk songs?"

"Of course!"

Being the only customers certainly had many benefits.

While we tucked into a steaming, fragrant stew, the brunette kept appearing at my elbow to update me on her quest for an hotel. By the time we had got to pudding, she returned with good news.

"*Oospyech!*" (Success!) She had located an hotel nearby which had hot water and telephones, and which would cost £15 per night per person.

"Is that all right?" she enquired.   Her original triumph at finding somewhere for us to stay was suddenly overlaid by her fear that £15 a night might be too expensive for such scruffy foreigners.

"Yes, yes, excellent," I assured her. "Thank you very much for all your trouble."

As we got up to leave, the final kindness:

"Oleg here will drive to the hotel. You follow him, OK?"

"OK! Thank you again."

We climbed back into the Toyota and followed Oleg in his battered white van to our goal – a perfectly ordinary looking hotel. But it provided luxury beyond our wildest dreams – our room had a loo, a bath and a shower. Norman drove back to his lonely billet at the Olympic Stables while Mary and I gave our filthy clothes to the *dijornaya* (floor manageress), with profuse and embarrassed explanations as to why everything was so dirty.

It was 10.30 p.m., but I couldn't have a bath as there was no hot water left.

So we were not quite back in the West yet.

We discovered the following day, not entirely to our surprise, that Minsk was famous for its linen. So while Norman settled into his room, Mary and I walked to the centre of the old town and found a linen shop.

"Look at this beautiful table cloth!" Mary exclaimed.

"I'm so glad you like it," I answered, laughing, "because now I can at last buy you a belated birthday present!" After some discussion, I added some napkins to the table cloth, and bought ten metres of wonderfully thick, soft cream-coloured linen, out of which Mary offered to make me a dressing gown.

Back at the hotel it was time for lunch. This was "Veat booyion with huff past." Hum. Whatever it was, it was pretty tasteless, and the chips that came with it were cold – and the bill that also came with it was a whopping £38 for the three of us!

I realised to my dismay that, in spite of the lack of hot water the previous night, we were no longer in wild places. The lobby was full of Germans, and I was able to pay with my credit card.

Even the rubbish beside the roads had changed from discarded mediaeval agricultural implements and native vodka bottles to empty packets of Marlboro cigarettes and bottles that had contained expensive Scotch. There were also increasing numbers of foreign-registered lorries – we spotted several Dutch ones, a couple from Teheran, and one removal van from Cheltenham – and expensive western cars such as Mercedes and BMW.

Mary and I mourned the passing of real Russia, but Norman, who had the unenviable task of doing the shopping, was absolutely thrilled to be able to go into a shop with a fair chance of finding something he wanted to buy.

I telephoned my husband to update him on our progress, and told him that we would be at the Polish border within a week.

"I'll meet you there!" Andrew was enthusiastic. "What can I bring?"

"Oh great – thank you. We need warm clothes, please – Mary and I were absolutely frozen in Bryansk, and although the weather is much milder here, it's bound to get colder as we go along. And could you possibly get me a waterproof riding coat? We also need some more horse shoes."

"No problem. It will be wonderful to see you again!"

We packed up and drove out to the stables. My horses looked well and relaxed, and I walked into the director's office and paid for their keep (£2 per horse per day, in roubles). He was in a meeting, so I kept it brief.

"Thank you so much for looking after my horses," I said.

"*Nyet problyem!* (No problem.) What are you doing in Minsk? If you are going to England, you should have gone in a straight line through Gomel."

"They told us it was too dangerous to go through Gomel!"

"Dangerous? Why?"

"After Chernobyl," I explained.

The director and his colleagues roared with laughter.

"No, no, it's not dangerous at all!"

To this day, I have no idea if I was wise to avoid the fallout area, or foolish to have added several hundred miles to our journey.

A couple of rainy days later Mary and I turned a corner to find our truck parked outside … a motorway café!

"I don't know whether to be pleased at the prospect of a hot meal or sad at yet another sign that every day brings us closer to civilisation!" I remarked to Mary, as we pulled the saddles off and tethered the horses on the verge.

"Frankly, Barbara, I just want to go home. I don't know how much longer I can stand Norman's presence." Mary was tight-lipped, so I said no more.

That afternoon brought the most frightening moment of all. We were trudging along the main road in a cocoon of cold, wet misery when Pompeii freaked out completely at an oncoming, overtaking lorry and tried to fling himself under its gargantuan wheels, and for a heart-stopping few seconds I thought I was about to die. Somehow I managed to drive him back onto the verge.

"That was close!" I said to Mary as my heart pounded wildly. "Thank God you were leading Muffin."

"Yes, it was lucky. We have to get off this damned road."

Unfortunately the countryside we were riding through was very marshy, so staying off the damned road meant taking tracks which took us miles out of our way.

Norman stayed on the road, and we used the walkie-talkies to make contact until we got back to the highway. A massive forest loomed ahead.

"Look, girls, you are going to have to stay on the road for a while now."

"There must be tracks through the forest," I said optimistically. "Honestly, it just isn't safe on the road – even for the mares, who are totally bomb-proof in traffic – the lorries hurtle past so fast and so close."

"She's right," Mary added firmly. "It's just too bloody dangerous."

Norman was annoyed – it would have been much easier for him to have us on the road where he could see us. But he could have had no idea, from the safety of the truck, how truly frightening it was to be on horseback in that situation.

So Mary and I plunged into the gloomy pine forest. As I had foreseen, there were tracks aplenty. Everything was fine until we decided that we needed to turn south and head back for the road. What I had not foreseen was that those tracks led us in any direction except southwards. For two hours we blundered around among the dark conifers, desperately seeking a track going the right way. We could not just set off on a compass bearing because the ground between the tracks was swamp.

"This is terrible," I called to Mary, "I feel like Alice through the Looking Glass! Are we *ever* going to find a way out of this wretched place?"

"I honestly don't know. Let me try to radio Norman."

That didn't help, of course, as neither could tell where the other was.

The sun was going down fast and it was getting darker by the minute. As we rode, I considered the possibility that we might not find a way out before night fell completely.

We wouldn't die, of course. It was raining, not snowing or freezing. There were unlikely to be wolves or bears prowling around so close to a busy road. We could tie the horses to the trees and just sit there, wet and hungry, until the morning. But I did not relish the prospect.

"Look, Mary! This track is heading south!"

We turned onto it, our hearts in our mouths. Would it take us back to the road, or would it crush our hopes by suddenly turning in another direction, as so many others had done?

We were in luck! After barely a quarter of a mile we found ourselves in a yard bordered by houses and barns, beyond which was the road!

"Look, can you radio Norman and stand beside the road so he can find you? I'll see if there are any stables here."

One of the houses had a lighted window, so I jumped off Pompeii, walked up to the door and banged on it.

"*Dobry vyetcher* (good evening)" I said politely to the woman who opened it. "I am English, can you please help us?"

The woman, Lyuba, was all smiles and warmly welcoming. Behind her I could see an office with three or four burly men working at desks.

"Could we please put our horses and our car in that barn?" and I pointed at the biggest one.

"I'm sorry, it's locked."

I must have looked terribly disappointed, because one of the men got up and came to the doorway.

"Well, there are three empty stables you can use," he said. "And you can sleep next to the stove in our office here, if you like."

"Oh wonderful – thank you so much!"

By now Norman had found Mary and they had come over to join me. The stables were so small that Masha, the biggest horse, had to be reversed into her stall as she would never have been able to turn round in it. But Lyuba showed us where to find some hay, and in no time at all the horses were warm and dry, tucking into their oats.

"Now, you must stay with me!" our hostess insisted.

"Oh please don't worry, we'll be perfectly all right in the office."

"No, no. Look, there is my house right next door. Come."

We followed meekly.

"This is my husband, Edvard," she indicated a drunk slumped in an armchair.

"*Ochin pryatna*" (pleased to meet you) I said as I shook his hand.

Between his thick local accent and slurred speech, I could only understand about a tenth of what Edvard said. But it didn't seem to matter.

Mary and I peeled spuds while Lyuba milked the cow, and we sat down to a delicious hot meal.

After supper, Mary started writing her diary. Mary is left-handed.

Lyuba and Edvard were shocked and horrified.

"Look! Look! She's using the wrong hand!" They said that in much the same tone they might have used to say, "She's a Satanist!"

"What do you mean, 'the wrong hand'? Lots of people in England use that hand – even my daughter! Don't you know anybody who writes with their left hand?"

"No, of course not! It is crazy! Nobody – it is not possible to write with the left hand!"

"Well, my friend does!" But I said no more.

The horses needed shoeing again. Indeed, Pompeii was slightly lame on one of his front legs, so I had switched over to riding Muffin.

One day I was being cross-examined by a herd of ancient Belarussian women, all identically dressed in many layers of cheap clothes and with their heads warmly wrapped in headscarves. They were much less backward in coming forward than their Russian cousins.

"You know, of course, that we can speak Polish?" one of them asked.

"Polish? How come?"

"This used to be Poland!"

"You're joking?"

"No, of course not. Look at the gravestones!"

"Gravestones? What do you mean?" I was really puzzled now.

"You will see that the names of the dead are all carved in Latin writing, not Cyrillic characters."

My ignorance was a disgrace. A post-war baby, I had never been told that Poland had been moved about 50% eastwards after the Nazis had been defeated. Belarus, from the current border almost as far as Minsk, had once been Poland, whereas the port of Gdansk, I learned much later, had once been part of Germany and known as Danzig.

As we rode through one village, a local bloke came galloping up to ask us where we'd got our saddles.

"From England!"

"How did you get them?" He lolled on the back of his horse, looking astounded.

"We are English."

"Impossible! If you're English, how is it you speak Russian?"

"I learnt it for the occasion." What else could I say? But I wanted to interrogate him.

"Is there a farrier nearby? Our horses, especially this stallion, need new shoes."

"We have no shoes."

"I know. That's OK, we have the shoes. We just need somebody to put them on for us."

"I have a friend who can do that."

The friend, for no good reason that we could see, refused to put a shoe on Pompeii. As we turned away, puzzled, his friends persuaded him to change his mind, and with great reluctance he put a new shoe on Pompeii's near fore[11].

Although I was holding the stallion while the press-ganged farrier worked on him, he must have done something wrong. Perhaps he trimmed the frog? For the next two weeks Pompeii, to my great concern, walked with very short steps.

Next time, I mused, next time I'll learn to trim hooves and shoe the horses myself. *Next time?* Don't be ridiculous, I chided myself, you haven't even finished this journey yet, how can you already be thinking about *next time*?

But I was. I already knew that as soon as I got home I'd get fidgety feet and start pouring over maps.

Our next landmark was Grodna, almost at the Polish border, where Norman managed to find some stables and an hotel.

The hotel boasted a discotheque, so I danced the night away.

And woke up with a hangover.

A day later we arrived in Poland.

---

[11] Front left foot.

CHAPTER 19 – POLAND WITH MARY

The border between Russia and Belarus having mysteriously disappeared, Belarus to Poland was our first frontier crossing, and I was rather anxious about it.

We arrived to find a long queue of cars, vans, trucks and lorries, all patiently waiting to go through. None of the drivers seemed to mind that we on our horses barged straight to the front, closely escorted by Norman in the truck. The border guards were in the process of changing shifts, so we settled down to wait patiently beside the twenty-foot high wire fence. There was plenty of grass, so the horses grazed peacefully.

An hour later we were approached by an obviously senior, very Prussian-looking officer, escorted by three underlings. To my surprise, he addressed me in English.

"What makes you think you are allowed to take these horses out of Belarus?" he barked.

"We have permission," I answered meekly.

"Permission? What permission?" He seemed determined not to let us through.

"Well, we have permission to enter Poland, and I paid the duty on the horses back in Ooryoopinsk," I said, rather more firmly.

"Show me the documents!" I was not accustomed to being treated in such a high-handed way, but I concealed my annoyance as Norman produced the file.

The Very Important Man scrutinised the file with the greatest of care, obviously hoping that we had failed to acquire one of the necessary pieces of paper. Fortunately for me, we had everything we needed.

"Everything is in order," he muttered in Russian to one of his minions, "she has paid her dues. Let them through."

Well, well, well, I thought. Anna Shubkina actually did obtain all the necessary paperwork. It should not have cost me anything like the $3,500 she had demanded, but at least my documents were in order – I could have paid that much money and still not had everything I needed to take the horses into Poland.

We went through to the next stage: I was grilled by a fat, pasty Customs official while a charming woman, the border vet, inspected our veterinary certificates. As is so often the case, she did not even glance at the horses themselves! Her job was quickly completed, but the greasy

Customs man made us wait while he played backgammon. For four hours.

Eventually we were graciously permitted to cross No Man's Land into Poland.

Hurrah – we've made it across the first frontier! I thought.

There was Andrew, waving frantically, and they let him through while his taxi driver was despatched to find and bring back the duty vet. More waiting.

The sun had struggled through the early-morning mist and we were resigned to yet another delay. The horses were not quite so relaxed, however, as we were now officially in Poland, so instead of endless stretches of waste ground full of grass, there were flower-beds and shrubs and suchlike – not for equine consumption.

"Darling, you look absolutely wonderful! I was expecting you to be thin, pale and exhausted – instead you're healthy and glowing!" Andrew did look genuinely astonished.

"Really? Well, I am probably even thinner than usual, but for the past three or four months I've lived the healthiest outdoor life imaginable. Why on earth did you expect me to look pallid and wan?"

"Well, I don't know. I certainly thought you'd be exhausted."

"There have been times when I've been terribly tired, but that was mainly in the early days."

"Whatever – this life obviously suits you," Andrew remarked. "And look, I've brought you a mobile telephone so you can stay in touch."

"I don't think it'll work here. But thank you very much."

"No, probably not, but it should work once you get to Germany, and maybe even on the western fringes of Poland? And obviously you can use it in England."

In due course the vet appeared, signed all our documents, and we rode to a local veterinary surgery where blood samples were taken from all the horses for Andrew to take back to England. Pompeii, Masha and Muffin were then led into the most sumptuous loose boxes they had ever seen.

"They are having a very easy time of it!" I told Andrew. "We've only averaged about fifteen or twenty miles a day for the last three or four days!"

"Only? Seems quite a lot to me!"

"Not when they're so fit, and have all day to do it in!"

But Andrew was no horseman, so it meant nothing to him.

The following day Norman drove Andrew to Warsaw airport, and he flew back to England, clutching the all-important blood samples.

We got back into the saddle and carried on.

Poland proved to be linguistically interesting and challenging. In some respects Polish is similar to Russian, but many of the most important words are completely different. In addition, I never really got the hang of the spelling, and had to write new words phonetically using the Cyrillic script, while concealing this embarrassing fact from the Poles.

Poland was also a tricky country from a diplomatic point of view. Having been invaded by the French, the Russians and the Germans, finding a common language that did not offend the listener was fraught with difficulties. After a while I learnt the Polish for, "Excuse me, I am English. Do you speak English? French? German? Russian?"

From a horseman's standpoint Poland was a sad disappointment. There was a huge number of fences and ditches which prevented us from taking the shortest line across country, or even take to the safety of a grassy verge. In this respect Poland had more in common with cosy little England than it did with its giant neighbour.

Geographically, however, Poland was breathtaking. The countryside was stunningly beautiful, with glorious forests; dressed now in their fiery autumn foliage, undulating hills and picturesque Alpine lakes.

From the shopping point of view, Poland was heaven!

"Do you know," Mary said as we rode along one day, "that yesterday I managed to buy bread, *and* tomatoes, *and* milk – all in the same shop and on the same day!"

"Really? That's amazing!" And we looked at each and giggled. Our values and attitudes had changed so much.

The weather was an improvement for a while. Dahlias still flowering in the gardens we passed proved that there had been no frost yet, although by now it was the middle of October. And while we had been soaked or frozen for most of the previous few weeks, we were now basking in glorious sunshine during the day, and sitting round the campfire at night still wearing only T-shirts and jodhpurs.

It was in Poland that my planned route went dramatically awry.

My original idea had been to go in a straight line – obvious, really. Then I had had to agree to a wide loop to avoid the Ukraine and Chernobyl. But I still had it in mind to go straight across the middle of

Poland, into Germany and straight across that country, and finally into The Netherlands.

The many delays had, however, caused me to reconsider the final part of the journey, and I had decided to head for Hamburg and take a ferry to England from there instead of from The Hook of Holland.

Now everyone I met swore blind that I would not be permitted to ride through Germany. That is to say, I would be allowed to ride during the day, but it seemed that camping during the winter was strictly forbidden. Whether or not that advice was correct, Mary had announced that she would have to go home soon, so I was going to be riding alone with three horses – not a task lightly to be undertaken on busy German roads.

At one lunch-break I discussed the situation with the team. When we looked at the map, I was surprised to discover that Sweden was only a short hop across the Baltic from the north coast of Poland. While we talked, Norman poured us all a drink – although lunchtime boozing was something we never, ever did.

"Why don't you just put the horses on a lorry and drive through Germany?" Norman wanted to know.

"No way! I said I'd ride them home, and that's what I'm going to do," I responded heatedly, horrified at the thought of cheating.

"Why don't you take the ferry from Gdansk to Ystad in Sweden?" asked Mary. "Then you could ride from Ystad to Gothenburg before taking the ferry to Harwich."

Mary had lived in Sweden for a while, and had good friends there.

I was tempted. Not only would Sweden probably have plenty of forest tracks and not too many main roads, but there is also a law there which states that travellers are allowed to camp anywhere for two nights.

'Well, I suppose we could find out...."

So it was that we headed north towards Gdansk instead of continuing our eternal trek westwards.

We found an hotel, and telephone calls to Andrew were followed by a flurry of frantic faxes flying back and forth to England, Gdansk and the Swedish Board of Agriculture.

It was only when we finally arrived in Gdansk that we discovered that the Gdansk-Ystad ferry, so clearly marked on my map, had either been withdrawn or ran only in summer. Fortunately we had found some wonderful lodgings for us and for the horses at the Sopot Hippodrome, so at least we had access to telephones as well as to running water.

And we took the opportunity to ride the horses into the sea! Predictably, they were at first terrified of the waves, but they soon lost their fear as we cantered through the water.

Now I had a problem. Mary was definitely leaving and I could not get across to Sweden. Or rather, I could not reach Sweden from Gdansk. I'd have to ride across the rest of Poland and take a ferry from Swinoujscie to Ystad.

A telephone call home solved the first problem.

"Katie, darling, can you get a couple of weeks off work to ride across Poland with me?"

"Oh! I'd love to! I'll see what I can do - I'm owed some holiday. Where are you? I'll ring you back tomorrow."

So while I did battle with assorted bureaucrats and smarmy officials, my darling daughter braved her boss and succeeded in wheedling ten days' leave with immediate effect.

I still cannot believe how complicated it is to take horses across a modern border! If I am driving a car, nobody inspects it to check that the brakes, for example, are working. For that matter, nobody checks me to ensure that I am not infected with Hepatitis, AIDS, or TB.

So why are horses so different? Mine had passports and they had veterinary certificates to prove they were not carrying any dangerous equine diseases.

In addition, there were only specified border points where horses were allowed to cross.

Why?

Any vet would be able to check them, take a blood sample and analyse it, so why were we not free to ride across frontiers at any point we chose?

My plans changed almost on a daily basis, from trying to get into Germany and riding across it, in spite of the warnings I had received, to taking a ferry to Sweden from Swinoujscie. Everyone I met had a firm view as to the best way for me to get home, and each new opinion contradicted the last one.

If my departure had not been so dreadfully delayed by the wretched Anna Shubkina I would not have encountered all these problems, which were caused mainly by the fact that it was October, not August.

Frankly, I did not know what was the best way to proceed, but I reasoned with my usual optimism that everything would work out in the end.

CHAPTER 20 – POLAND WITH KATIE

Mary left us at Gdansk, and we hugged each other tightly as we said farewell. Although I was sorry she was going, I was looking forward to seeing Katie again, and I hoped that the atmosphere would be lighter once Mary and Norman were no longer forced into each other's company.

The next day we drove to the airport to meet Katie. Norman had never met her, and it was amusing to see him so plainly impressed by the very pretty, slim brown-eyed blonde who emerged from Customs, rushed over and embraced me. It was wonderful to see her again – and what a good traveller she was, arriving as she did with just one small knapsack.

We were up at 4.30 the following morning, ready to ride on, only to be greeting by a frosty, clear dawn.

Poor Katie! She certainly got thrown in at the deep end.

Katie is, like me, a horsewoman to the bone, but she had experimented with different branches of riding: a year as a stable lass in Newmarket had left her with a taste for speed, while a stint working in a polo yard had given her yet another perspective on horses.

What she had never done was to ride across country, negotiating obstacles as and when she encountered them, and with no idea where nightfall would find us. I, on the other hand, had spent three months getting to know my horses and learning exactly how much I could expect of them. This included clambering up and down terrain that I would never have had the courage to do in an English landscape.

Katie set off riding Masha while I rode Pompeii and led Muffin, and within a few hours my daughter had her first experience of the strange "techniques" one occasionally resorts to on an expedition.

We were riding through a pretty golden forest alongside a railway line which took us safely under a motorway but which then went over a very long, narrow bridge across a dirt track. With no idea when the next train was due, I decided not to risk picking our way between the sleepers for a quarter of a mile, but to bail out onto the trail below.

"Can you hold Muffin, please, sweetheart?" I jumped off Pompeii, handed the grey's rope to Katie, and together Pompeii and I slid down a fifteen-foot embankment.

Katie let out an anguished wail of, "Mummy!!" as my stallion and I disappeared over the edge.

A bewildered old Polish couple was equally horrified to find a horse and a woman appearing out of nowhere and landing on their path.

"Could you please hold him for me?" I asked, holding out the reins. Instinctively the old man took them, and I struggled back up the near-vertical slope.

"What on earth are you doing?" Katie was stunned.

"We can't go across that bridge, so we'll have to take that track down there. Here, give me Muffin, and jump off."

I took Muffin's lead rope and she and I repeated the manoeuvre I had just executed with Pompeii, leaving Katie and Masha to make their own way down.

"Thank you so much!" I smiled gratefully at the bemused locals as I took Pompeii's reins back and swung into the saddle. I turned to Katie. "Are you OK darling?"

She laughed. "Yes thank you! But I did wonder what on earth you were up to!"

We continued, chatting away like magpies. While I had been in Russia Katie had met a wonderful man, Richard, and as we rode along she told me all about him. He was perfect in every way, they loved each other to pieces, and surely this was The One!

And so we thoroughly enjoyed each other's company while sauntering through the picturesque Polish countryside, cantering through deciduous forests, and skirting enchanted lakes.

But there were still some dangers to come.

Two days later we were riding through a thick pine forest, following a major railway line. Norman had to stay on the roads, and we had arranged to meet at a level crossing about ten miles further on.

We picked our way through thick fog along a very faint track. Every now and again we had to skirt a bog, or jump a fallen tree or a ditch. Because of the very poor visibility, we did not dare stray too far from the railway. Enormous dark conifers reared up all around us, adding to the sense of gloom. It was eerily silent and very scary.

And the walkie-talkie's battery was flat.

"Are you sure we're going the right way?" Katie asked, somewhat nervously, after several hours.

"No, not really! Except that the railway line is still over there on the left. If we stick close to it, then logically we can't help but arrive at the level crossing."

Logic is, however, the first casualty of fear. I knew in my head that we were in no danger at all, that in due course we would come to the road on which Norman would be parked, waiting for us.

But deep inside me a primitive voice said, "You could be lost forever in this forest! The wolves will find you before Norman does! You, your precious daughter, your horses – you're all doomed."

I pulled myself together, made a joke of it, and within half an hour we stumbled onto the road. There was Norman, patiently waiting. We were safe.

Four days from Gdansk we arrived in Bialy Bor, where Norman had booked the horses into some "military" stables for the night. To my amazement there were no less than eighty aristocratic stallions kept in magnificent buildings that would have done justice to Buckingham Palace.

We crept in, as scruffy as ever, hoping at first that nobody would sneer at my very working-class horses. Then I remembered what these so-called "working-class" horses had done, and realised that we could all be proud of our achievement so far, not embarrassed by our lack of breeding.

We humans checked into a small local *pension*.

"Hey, I feel just like Crocodile Dundee!"

Katie was luxuriating in a hot shower while simultaneously washing her underwear.

"I'll never take hot running water for granted again," I agreed. "Nor dry clothes."

"When you get home you may not bother to take a shower for days on end, on the grounds that you've already had one this month. On the other hand, perhaps you'll have a bath every hour, just because it's possible!"

"I'm more worried about the loo, frankly."

"What do you mean?"

"Well, since leaving Moscow I haven't had access to a 'water closet' more than half a dozen times – it's either been an earth box, or a bush deep in the woods. I may well have got out of the habit of flushing!"

Winter had resumed with a vengeance, and we were getting colder and wetter each day. Worse: the truck kept getting stuck in boggy tracks, and it frequently took several hours to release it.

While this meant the horses were able to rest and graze, I grew increasingly impatient and irritable at wasting travelling time, not to mention struggling with branches and twigs in an effort to get the truck out of trouble. The purpose of the journey was, after all, to get the horses to England, not to spend so much time extricating the vehicle which was supposed to help me.

In addition, there had been dozens of occasions when we riders had been forced to hang around beside the roads, usually in driving rain, waiting for Norman to find us. While it is true that he was able to go and make telephone calls and do the shopping, not to mention carry the oats in the truck, by this stage of the journey I had come to the conclusion that the negative side far outweighed the positive.

I caught myself thinking that 'next time' I would not take any motorised back-up.

Next time!

After a very happy eight days riding with my daughter, we arrived in Lobez, where we found stables for the horses at a stud there, and rooms for ourselves.

We spent a jolly few days there, dancing and drinking with both Poles and Belgians. One snowy morning Katie and I were lent two stallions so we could join the *Hubertus*. This involved galloping through the forest, following a trail marked with red ribbons. Riders could jump man-made obstacles if they chose, none of them very large. Although Katie and I had obviously elected to take the jumping route, neither of our stallions had any brakes, so we had quite a struggle on our hands. But it was great fun!

At 2 p.m. we all had a break for barbecue and vodka in the snow. It was all very civilized: while we riders clustered around a massive bonfire, grooms walked the horses around for us.

To my great sadness, it was time for Katie to return to England, as she had the carrot of wanting to get back to Richard and the stick of having the rent to pay.

So the three of us climbed into the truck and headed through the snow to Berlin airport.

I loathe airports and farewells with almost equal intensity.

Surrounded by uncaring, hurrying strangers, I hugged my daughter tightly.

"Bye bye darling. It's been wonderful riding with you. I hope you weren't too cold and uncomfortable?"

"No, no. I've really enjoyed it, thank you. I was cold sometimes, but only because my sleeping bag wasn't as good as yours! I hope the rest of the journey goes well, and that you get Pompeii, Masha and Muffin safely home soon."

"Mmmm – me too. I'll keep you posted. Say 'hi' to Richard for me, and tell him I said he was a very lucky man!"

"Mummy, really! Have you got any messages for Andrew?"

"Oh!" I'd forgotten Andrew. Which was unkind, as I knew he was doing everything he could to help me. "No, I don't think so. Just tell him I'll ring whenever I can and let him know how wildly my planned itinerary has changed! OK – now go before I start crying."

I waved and smiled through my tears as my little girl threaded her way through the crowds before disappearing from sight. It had been fun with her. My marriage to her father had disintegrated when she was six months old, so Katie and I had become very tight and the best of friends.

Back in Lobez I continued trying to figure out what to do for the best. Well-meaning people had bombarded me with advice, all of it contradictory, about where, when and how I could cross into Germany. As I could not verify anything I was told, I decided that I would definitely take the ferry from Swinoujscie to Ystad in Sweden and ride up to Gothenburg.

Two young women I had met at the stables in Lobez, Edita and Yola, begged to be allowed to accompany me for the first two days – our last two days in Poland. We had been invited to spend the night with a delightful couple called George and Alice who lived in a tiny village called Imno.

My horses came charging out of their stables: well-fed and rested, they were raring to go. They were still rather thin, especially by Polish standards, and I had grown rather irritated at having to defend them.

"Your horses are much too thin!"

"Yes, I know they're thin, but you can see they are very healthy!"

"No, no, a horse should be much fatter than that."

"Yes, your horses are fatter than mine, but only because they are a much heavier type of horse. After all, Pompeii and his mares have travelled for more than three thousand kilometres."

"And *you* are too thin!"

"Well, I have travelled the same distance, too. And I am also very healthy."

Thin or not, my horses covered thirty-two miles that day, through what had now become a familiar but never-boring landscape. It was bitterly cold, but late-autumn foliage still clung tenaciously to the trees. As Pompeii jogged along, I drank in the vivid blue sky, the golden leaves, the frosty grass.

"It won't be long now before we're home," I told him.

"Home? I thought we were gypsies, would travel forever and never get 'home'!"

"Silly boy. I'm not a gypsy! One of these days you and the mares will be led into a large, warm and comfortable stable, which will be home for the rest of your life."

Little did I know then that this was not to be.

But I did wonder how long it would take the horses to realise that they had arrived, that our journey was over. The longest they had ever spent in one place since we set off was three weeks in Stari Oskol.

We arrived at Imno to find a journalist called Richard waiting for us, and after we had posed for the camera we settled the horses into nice, warm dry stables. They were quite small stables, as George and Alice bred Shetland ponies, but my three Cossacks were delighted. There was only one small snag – Pompeii's lodgings were round the corner from those of his mares, so he could neither see them nor smell them.

"Where are you, girls????" he bellowed at the top of his lungs.

Silence. The mares had obviously decided to keep quiet and let Pompeii worry about them.

"Where have you gone? Are you there?" The stallion's neighing increased in volume and desperation.

Silence.

I took him a hay net and some oats.

"Where are my mares?" He pranced around the little loose-box, agitated but not so frantic that I feared he would try to leap over the stable door.

"Don't worry, they're close by. Here, eat this," I reassured him as I hung up the hay net.

"Are you sure they are here? Why do they not answer?" But he was settling down and started guzzling his oats.

"You'll see them tomorrow. They are here, I promise."

And I walked round to feed the naughty mares too.

"Why don't you reply and let him know you are here?"

"Ha! Ha" giggled Muffin. "We thought it would be funny!"

"I don't care," sighed Masha. "What's the point of making friends when we're all doomed anyway?" And she pulled a wisp of hay out and chewed on it listlessly.

We had planned to ride the next day to the home of yet another helpful Pole, called Veronica, before loading up the horses and heading for the ferry terminal.

Over breakfast, however George made a suggestion.

"For the sake of a few miles only, why don't you box the horses up here and have them driven onto the ferry at Swinoujscie? There's no point in riding twelve miles just for the sake of it!"

He looked at me keenly – he was a very intense person. Tall and dark, he was the perfect foil to his wife, Alice, who was small, gentle and frail.

"Well…. I hate to cheat, but it does seem a bit silly to cover such a short distance just to prove a point! Especially as the animals have to be put on a lorry for the ten miles leading to the ferry terminal. If you don't mind us staying another day, then yes, that's an excellent idea."

"You can stay as long as you like!" George, like all the kind people we had met in Poland, was infinitely hospitable. "And it will give you plenty of time to give a long interview to our journalist friend, Basha!"

"Basha? My name is Barbara!"

"Of course, but here in Poland we often give the nickname 'Basha' to people called 'Barbara'."

The name stuck. Since then everybody, including my Swiss mother (who obviously had me christened) has called me Basha.

While Norman drove Edita and Yola back to Lobez, I was being interrogated by the journalist.

Small and dapper, with a neat moustache and a battered pork-pie hat. Richard sat at the kitchen table looking like a spiv on a racecourse.

"Now, tell me all about your adventures!" he cried, rubbing his hands together in anticipation of a litany of lurid tales.

Half an hour later he was drooping with disappointment. I refused to invent any thrilling episodes just to make his readers happy, and I down-played the frightening parts, such as the attempted rape on the farm and the problem with the drunken hooligans. In the end, I told him what I thought was important.

"Richard, the point here is not the reality of the danger. The point is that the danger has been an ever-present possibility for the whole of the last three months. Before I left England, I faced up to this potential danger, and accepted it. As so often happens, however, once you accept the likelihood of danger, and do not run away from it, that danger never materialises."

The next morning, Vincent, a Belgian, drove up in a very rickety lorry to take my horses to Sweden.

My real problems were just beginning.

CHAPTER 21 – SWEDEN, A BUREAUCRATIC NIGHTMARE

"OK, boys and girls.   Here we go – nothing to worry about!" I soothed with false blandishments. In reality I was extremely nervous.

Pompeii peered in disgust at the rotten and wobbly loading ramp towards which I was leading him.

"You want me to walk on *that*?" he asked incredulously.

"Yes. It will be OK. Don't tread here, or here," I instructed him as we stepped onto the ramp together, trying to keep him away from the actual holes.

Why had I not inspected the lorry first? I cursed my stupidity. I would never have agreed to load my horses onto this flimsy contraption. But it was too late to find another one and still catch the ferry.

With Pompeii tied up, it was Masha's turn.

There were never any difficulties with Masha. She would go anywhere, do anything, while waiting for the inevitable. Death.

Muffin next.

"Oh come on, Muffin."   She was understandably reluctant, and baulked.

"But…. I don't like this stable at all!"

"I know, you just have to be brave, for a change. Look, Masha's there. Do you want to be left behind forever?"

That did it. Muffin hesitated for another few seconds, then launched herself into the lorry, causing it to shake alarmingly. We tied her up too, and quickly put up the ramp before the horses changed their minds. I climbed in the front and sat next to Vincent.

The drive to the ferry was the worst I have ever endured.

Vincent drove like a complete maniac.   Until relatively recently, Belgians did not have to take a driving test. I remembered Danielle, one of my Belgian girlfriends from school, getting into her parents' car on her eighteenth birthday and driving to the cinema. She'd never had a lesson in her life!

Fortunately the law changed some time in the 1970s.

But Belgians over the age of sixty have a reputation for being extremely unsafe behind the wheel, and to this day, if I see a car with the tell-tale Belgian red and white number-plate, I go onto the alert.

Vincent, with the incredibly precious cargo of my Cossack horses behind him, not only drove about 20 miles an hour faster than was safe, he also insisted on talking to me all the way, waving his hands around to emphasise particularly dramatic points.

"Vincent, please, please drive more slowly! These horses have never been in a lorry before." At least French was a language I spoke well, so there was no question of any misunderstandings on this occasion.

"More slowly?" Vincent was amazed. "You are not in a hurry?"

"No, Vincent. I am NOT IN A HURRY! In fact, could you please stop for a moment so I can see if the horses are all right."

Vincent, still looking astonished, pulled the lorry off the busy road and allowed me to run round to the little groom's door and check on my poor horses. They were standing there like angels, very quietly, but Pompeii was obviously petrified, as he was absolutely soaked in sweat.

He looked at me appealingly.

"For God's sake, get me out of here! What the hell is happening?"

The mares nodded in agreement.

"We don't like this. We're frightened. Can we come out now, please?"

"Not quite yet, but soon. Just be good for a while longer, I beg you."

I told them that in good faith – I had no idea then that the three horses were going to be stuck in that box for a total of fourteen hours.

We had an excellent crossing to Sweden.

We arrived in Ystad to complete pandemonium.

Waiting to greet us were twenty journalists, but, although we had alerted the Swedish authorities to our arrival, there was no vet. Thanks to the intervention of the journalists, a vet was found and arrived on the quayside two hours later.

Blond, burly and bland, he was completely useless.

"I can't let your horses through."

"Why not?"

"Their passports do not identify them properly. Look, they give the name and the colour, but that's all!"

"But nobody told me this! Surely the official people in the EEC must know that Russian passports are like this?"

"I'm sorry. I have to follow the rules. Your horses must go into quarantine, and we will take blood samples."

So my poor equine friends were sealed into their box by a Customs official and driven away by Victor. They had about another fifty miles to go, with nobody to check Victor's dangerous driving.

Also at the quayside to meet us was Sirvi Rasberg, a long-standing friend of my husband Andrew, and who had stayed with us a couple of times in England.

"It's good to see you again – but I am so sorry about your animals!" she commiserated. Although she knew nothing about horses, Sirvi had gone to the trouble of finding stables for Pompeii and the mares, but of course this was now irrelevant as they had gone to the quarantine stables.

"Come on, let's go home. Follow me – that's my car there." Sirvi was pointing at a compact blue vehicle. Norman and I climbed into the Toyota and followed Sirvi's car to Simrishamn, her home town, a few miles away.

None of us had any idea – could have had any idea – that my precious horses were to be imprisoned for no less than seventeen days while I did battle with the Swedish authorities.

Unfortunately the bureaucrats were not interested in me or my horses, and put every imaginable difficulty in my path.

"Nobody can read the Russian veterinarian certificate," complained the local vet.

"But what diseases do you fear other than the ones for which the horses have been repeatedly tested?"

"None."

"Well, then, do you care if the horses were riddled with diseases when we left, as long as they are healthy now?"

"Er….. We have to complete the formalities."

The following day I made repeated but unsuccessful calls to the Agriculture Department in a town called Jönköping. The officials there were too busy to talk to me, and too important to return my calls.

When I rang Bernard van Goethem, the Chief Vet in Brussels, he was very nice, but said he would leave it to the Swedes to sort everything out.

So Norman and I drove to Jönköping to confront the unhelpful people there. We sat around for hours in a sleek, elegant but uninviting waiting room.

"You can take your horses through Sweden to Gothenburg on a lorry."

"But I don't want to put them in a lorry! The whole point of this journey is to do the whole thing on foot!"

"Too bad."

In the meantime, I discovered to my horror that the quarantine fees were SEK325 per horse per day, plus 25 percent tax – a total of about US$180 a day.

"That is daylight robbery!" I exclaimed. "I want to see the horses."

"That is not permitted – they are in quarantine!"

There were several reasons for my difficulties.

The Swedes were new to the European Community at the time, and were terrified of letting in some dreadful disease.

They are an exceptionally bureaucratic race.

There was at the time an outbreak of "Newcastle disease," which affects all birds and the Agriculture wallahs were busy enforcing the slaughter of thousands of farmyard fowl.

By now I had been in touch with several Swedish transport companies, who had pointed out an unforeseen obstacle – the weather. The sea between Gothenburg and Harwich, in England, might be very rough at that time of the year (November).

"Maybe you will not be able to load your horses onto the ferry when you get there, if the weather is bad. Horses cannot vomit, of course."

"Of course not. And if the sea is very stormy, they might very well hurt themselves." Then and there I realised that I would not be able to stick to my original plan of riding all the way home. I picked up the telephone to ring the officious officials at the Agricultural department.

"Could you please change my letter of authority so I can leave your country from the port of Malmö, please?"

"This is very inconvenient. Why?"

"Your own transport companies have urged me not to ship the horses from Gothenburg at this time of the year. And anyway, if the poor animals are to be stuck in a horse-box, why go so far north when we can just head south for England."

"Well, I will see if we can do this."

"Yes, please do. I must say that none of the vets in Sweden seem to have spared the slightest thought for the welfare of my horses."

And I slammed the receiver down, furious and frustrated.

Eventually we had all the necessary permits from the Government, and so Norman and I climbed into the truck and set off for the Customs Office at Ystad. We needed another document – of course!

Clutching our file – which had now assumed gargantuan proportions – we walked into the echoing, unwelcoming Customs Hall and explained our requirement to a burly, fair-haired and bearded official.

"You cannot obtain this form unless you get a 'transit paper'."

"All right, where do we get this paper?"

"It must be issued by the freight-forwarding agents."

It took us half an hour to find the agents. We walked up to the counter and posed our question to the dark, thin man standing carelessly behind it.

"Can you please issue a 'transit paper' so I can take my horses back to England?"

"Let me see."

He studied the file, and asked a few questions.

"No, I am sorry, we cannot issue this paper." He did not look sorry at all as he handed back my file, just totally disinterested.

"Why on earth not?"

"Because this situation is not in the book."

Frustrated, we returned to the Customs people.

"What now?" I demanded.

The blond man shrugged. "Without the 'transit paper' there is nothing we can do. The regulations….."

"Well, we can't stay here for the rest of our lives. Please see if you can find a way out of this absurd situation." Exasperated, I walked out.

We returned the following day. The unhelpful official of the day before had been replaced by a charming, intelligent young man who seemed willing to try and help.

"The only way I can see out of this *impasse* is for you to pay a 'bond' which will be returned once you are in England," he smiled reassuringly.

"Wonderful! Well, not wonderful that we have to pay," I laughed, "but that we may be able to get away at long last."

"How much did you pay for the horses?" he needed to know.

"One million roubles each," I told him.

"How much is that?"

"About US$600," I said.

"OK, that means you will have to pay US$900 for the three horses," he said as he punched numbers into his calculator.

"No, wait! Sorry, it has been so long since I worked things out in roubles. One million roubles is about $200 – but you can check the current rate if you like."

"No, no need." The calculator was brought out again. "You must pay a bond of US$300."

I handed over the money, and Norman and I left the Customs Hall satisfied that we could be on our way the next day. At last. But we were not to escape that easily.

The telephone rang half an hour before we were due to leave.

"Hello, this is Annica from the Agriculture Department."

"Yes?" I said cautiously, with a sense of foreboding.

"I have telephoned my opposite number in Germany to warn him of your arrival, and he says you may not take your horses through his country."

I was stunned.

"Why did you telephone him?"

"It was my duty," she announced triumphantly, and put the receiver down.

Running through my mind during this exasperating battle with the bureaucrats was a serious worry.

Several years earlier, I had read a horrific story in the British newspapers. I could not recall the details, except that the leader of a Central Asian country had presented the Swedish Prime Minister with a very valuable Akhal-Teke stallion.

At vast expense the stallion had been flown by the Swedish Air Force to Stockholm.

When he arrived in Stockholm, his papers were inspected by the same wretched authorities with whom I was negotiating. These papers were not correct in some minor way.

The expensive horse had been shot.

Desperate now to get out of Sweden and avoid a similar fate for my poor equine companions who had brought me so far, I contacted Brussels again.

Bernard van Goethem and his colleague, Dietrich Russow, were absolutely appalled at my story.

"This is terrible!" I could almost hear them shaking their heads. "The Swedes should have let you in on a temporary permit. Have they taken blood samples?"

"Yes, they took them as soon as we got here."

"Have they analysed them?" Bernard van Goethem wanted to know.

"Not yet, although I keep asking them to do so."

"Apart from that, the Poles should have issued you with a proper Health Certificate, and the Germans have no reason whatsoever to refuse to let the horses through in a sealed horsebox."

As Monsieur van Goethem talked knowledgeably and reassuringly, I began to think that maybe we might get out unscathed after all.

"Leave it to us," he instructed, "and ring us back tomorrow."

I replaced the receiver with an immense sense of relief. Surely the Swedes would not dare destroy my horses now?

They did not.

Bernard van Goethem was the Chief Vet for the whole of the European Community, and so of course he outranked everybody! He decreed that the blood samples should be analysed immediately and, if negative, the Swedes should issue us with official documents which would enable us to travel freely anywhere within the European Community.

The blood samples were perfect.

When I rang to tell him how eternally grateful I was to him for saving my horses, he brushed off my thanks.

"Have you got the official EEC documents yet?"

"No, but I am assured they are being prepared. Are you certain there is no other form I might need?"

"Yes, quite certain. If you have that document you are free to travel anywhere provided you stay within European Community boundaries," he said warningly.

"Don't worry! After this experience I can assure you that I would never dream of trying to get into the EC again!"

That evening I had a telephone call from Thorleif, the driver of the horsebox I had booked.

"Is it true we are going on Wednesday?" he wanted to know.

"I have no idea – nobody has told me anything, as usual!" I moaned. "Where did you hear that?"

"Well, I had dinner with some friends in Malmö last night," Thorleif told me. "One of the other guests was Elizabeth Swensson."

"Who's she?" I didn't quite see what he was getting at.

"She is the local Official Veterinarian. And she'd never heard of you or your horses!"

"Oh my God! Do you have her telephone number?"

"Yes." I wrote it down, and thanked Thorleif for all his help.

I telephoned her the next day.

"No," she said, obviously mystified. "Nobody has said anything to me about the problems you are having. This is very strange, as the main part of my job is signing equine health certificates!"

"I can't believe it," I said. "Do you know Hans Andren, or Lars who took over from him?" These were the two local vets I had been in contact with.

"Yes, I know them. But Lars is impossible to work with. If you have any more problems, however, please let me know."

"I will," I promised. "And thank you!"

I hung up, puzzled. Had we been in Russia, all this incompetence would have been entirely normal. But I never expected such treatment in a western European country, least of all an efficient country such as Sweden.

Thanks to Bernard van Goethem the way was clear for us to leave. I rang to book the overnight ferry for Norman, me and the truck – not from Malmö as I had originally planned, but from Trelleborg to Travemunde in Germany. This was on Thorleif's recommendation, and he had already booked the crossing himself for the horsebox.

"What year were you and Mr Cross born?" the operator wanted to know.

I told her. But I was intrigued. Could it be that only people over a certain age were allowed to travel on that route? Or maybe only teenagers were permitted to go to Travemunde on Wednesdays?

"Why on earth do you want to know how old we are?" I could not resist asking.

"Oh, since the *Estonia* ferry sank, it was decided that it was necessary to know the ages of all the passengers."

"But I still don't understand why?"

"So that if there is a crisis, the elderly people can be located and helped to safety."

If the Swedish rule-makers could be that well-ordered, why on earth had they made such an unbelievable mess of my arrival?

At last, it was time to fetch the horses.

We said our farewells to Sirvi, who had uncomplainingly put up with having two people in her tiny flat for more than two weeks. We had done what we could to minimise the trauma, of course – cooking, washing-up, and taking Sirvi out to dinner from time to time. Norman had made himself extremely useful, too, by hanging pictures, putting up bookshelves and doing all the jobs that men traditionally do.

"Sirvi, I'll never be able to thank you enough!"

"Don't mention it – I enjoyed having you. It will be very quiet once you've gone! I hope you get your horses safely back to England."

Norman and I drove to the quarantine stables where Thorleif was waiting with the horsebox.

I paid the exorbitant sum of US$2,500 for seventeen days' quarantine, and the owner of the stables went to get Pompeii and the mares.

While we waited by the box, Thorleif took my arm.

"Have you ever had horses in quarantine before?" he enquired.

"No. Why?"

"When you see them, say nothing. You cannot do anything – just load them up and take them away. I have seen this situation a hundred times."

"What on earth are you talking about?"

"You'll see."

And when the horses were led out, I understood. Pompeii, Masha and Muffin, who had looked so well after their 2,500 mile trek, were in terrible condition. They were much thinner, their coats were dull and lifeless, and their heads drooped.

I gasped. For US$2,500 I had at least expected them to be properly fed.

Thorleif shot me a warning look, so I bit my tongue. We loaded the horses into stalls of deep golden straw in the lorry. Huge haynets were awaiting them, and the poor starving animals immediately started tearing at the hay.

I could not bring myself to speak to the man who had treated my horses in this terrible way. Gritting my teeth, hard, I waved farewell to Thorleif as the lorry rumbled slowly out of the yard, and I got into the Toyota.

"It's lucky we weren't here any longer," I said to Norman as he started the engine. "They'd have died of starvation!"

"You're exaggerating, as usual" he replied, "but they do look very poor."

We followed the horsebox to Trelleborg, and all the while I felt sick with apprehension in case the Swedes found yet another reason to keep us imprisoned. My worries were unfounded, and our ship set off for Travemunde dead on time.

CHAPTER 22 – HOME AT LAST

We were nearly there – finally! There was one more hiccough at Travemunde, where the German authorities held the lorry up for three hours in spite of the dozens of documents Thorleif showed them. Eventually they sealed the doors and reluctantly permitted the horsebox to proceed.

From this point on my magical journey degenerated into a media farce. As Norman drove the Toyota across Germany and into Holland, where we were going to take the ferry to England, my mobile telephone rang incessantly. For some reason my ride had caught the fancy of the press and the public, so I had my fifteen minutes of fame that day.

I very reluctantly agreed to sell my story to The Daily Express, one of Britain's tabloid newspapers. Although I still did not know exactly how precarious our financial situation was, I felt it was time to get some money back. Had I known, however, just how restricted we would be I would never have given an exclusive to any newspaper. When we arrived in England, the Daily Express team surrounded us like minders and refused to let any of the other reporters on the quayside take a photograph of the horses. They, poor beasts, were still confined to the box.

Mary had agreed to ride with me the 60-odd miles to our village, and had carefully planned a route which involved staying the night with William, a friend of hers. Unfortunately the press circus made it impossible for us to ride to William's, so the horses were driven there in their box while we humans went to an hotel nearby. That evening I told my story to The Daily Express.

"OK, tomorrow we'll mount up and ride the rest of the way home," I announced, when I had finished giving my account of the ride.

"Not bloody likely," said the Express reporter.

"What on earth do you mean?" I was mystified.

"You can't ride now – if anybody gets even one photograph of you and your horses during the next ten days, you can kiss goodbye to the money," he snarled.

"Well, I don't care! You've got your 'exclusive', you cheated me of one day's ride, you're not cheating me of my very last day in the saddle."

"It's your choice. Just remember, if we see a single photograph of you and the horses in any other newspaper, you'll get no money from us."

"So be it." I was very angry by now – I had been given to understand that an 'exclusive' meant that only that newspaper would get the full story. I had had no idea that all the other reporters, who had waited patiently at Harwich in the freezing cold, would only be permitted a few minutes' questioning.

We were up long before dawn the next day – the last day of November and six months to the day since I had left home.

"You can take this track here," William had informed us the night before, "which will lead you out the back of the farm. With a bit of luck, all the reporters will be waiting at the main entrance!"

This indeed turned out to be the case. Mary and I caught the horses with some difficulty, brushed them down quickly and tacked up Pompeii and Masha. It was still dark when we set off down the track which William had pointed out.

Andrew had volunteered to act as decoy, and spent most of the day driving around in my distinctive blue and black Mini, hotly pursued by the press hounds.

Mary and I just rode quietly along in the cold, misty dawn, hoping against hope that none of the other reporters would find us.

"I wonder how many extra copies of the newspaper they would have to sell to get back the money they paid me?" I wondered.

"How funny, I was just thinking the same thing!" Mary laughed.

"Plus they paid for the ferry crossing to Harwich, three bedrooms at an expensive hotel, and dinner!"

"Well, too bad if they lose money on it." Mary was unsympathetic, being as annoyed as I was at the high-handed treatment which had been meted out to us.

"The important thing is not to be seen," I cautioned.

We did get away with it in the end, but only because none of the reporters can have been horsemen.

Once we had reached the safety of the neighbouring farm, I let out a huge sigh of relief.

"If the newspapermen had drawn a line between where they knew we were last night, and where they knew we were going, we must have crossed that line a dozen times during the day!" Mary was jubilant.

"Obviously none of them knows anything about horses! They probably reasoned that racehorses gallop at about 40 m.p.h. Because we've been travelling between three and five miles an hour, they must have been looking in all the wrong places. Well, who cares why, my money is safe and I *did* get to ride the last 30 miles."

At that moment my mobile telephone rang.

"'Allo? Is that Basha?" a heavily-accented male voice wanted to know.

"Yes?"

"Ah! My name is Mikhail and I am London correspondent of *Izvestia*." I was impressed – this was one of Russia's best-known newspapers. (*Izvestia* means "news.")

"Oh yes, *Zdrastvoytye!*" I said.

"You speak Russian? Wonderful!" Mikhail said in tones of great relief, and started interrogating me in his native tongue. But we were very close to home, so after a few minutes I asked him to ring me again in an hour or so.

"That was really weird!" Mary exclaimed.

"What was?"

"Well, here we are all these months later, plodding through a misty English country park, and to hear you chattering away in Russian made me feel quite nostalgic."

"I know, in many ways I'm very sad that it's all over. This has become such a way of life, such a routine, that I really don't know how I am going to cope with being in the same place for the foreseeable future."

We turned into my stable yard, and put the horses in their new stables. They were, of course, quite unconcerned and started tearing at the hay which was waiting for them.

"How long do you think it will be before they realise they are now 'home' and we won't be moving on?" I wondered.

"God knows. What's the longest they've ever been in one place since you set out?"

"Um – three weeks in Stari Oskol," I replied. "So I suppose in a month or so they might begin to understand that we've stopped!"

I looked over the door at Pompeii, watching him contentedly munch on his hay. He turned his head when he saw me.

"We're arrived, sweetheart," I whispered. "This is it. No more travelling."

He looked sideways at me.

"Maybe," he said mysteriously.

Standing by his stable, I looked across at my home. It was an enchanting house, and I had poured a lot of love into it during the ten years we had been there.

But I had not missed it at all in the past six months. Studying it now, I realised it was nothing more than a pile of bricks into which I had stashed my many possessions.

I walked back down the path and went into the kitchen, where a delighted Andrew was on the telephone to all his friends.

Strangely, I felt no sense of triumph.

Achievement, yes – I had done what I had set out to do and brought all three horses safely back to England.

But triumph, no. After all, it had been a very tame trip and I had thoroughly enjoyed myself. I felt quite guilty at all the praise being heaped on my head hailing me as "courageous" and "intrepid."

Sadness. Yes, there was an indefinable sadness. Far from being happy to be 'home', I felt like a wild bird imprisoned in a gilded cage.

The next few weeks passed in a cyclone of activity.

The truck had to be unpacked, and everything put away.

The media was still interested in my little adventure. I accepted an invitation to appear on 'The Richard and Judy Show' on television, and on Selina Scott's television chat show.

I was instructed to "Bring one of the horses!"

"What?"

"Why not? We've had a tiger in the studio, and a donkey."

"Not at the same time, I trust!"

Pompeii being closest to my heart, and the most sensible, was designated as the TV star. On the first show he behaved impeccably.

Selina Scott's staff rang me a couple of days before we were due to appear.

"Just thought I'd mention that you'll have to put the horse in a lift to get him to the studio."

"Oh no! I can't possibly do that! This is a semi-wild stallion from the steppes, you know, not a meek dressage horse."

"Don't worry, it'll be fine – it's a goods lift, large and slow." I went to inspect it, and it was. Even so, I telephoned the horse transport company booked to bring Pompeii to London.

"Believe it or not, those lunatics at the TV station want me to put my horse in a lift!" I heard laughter at the other end of the line. "So please bring some kind of tranquilliser – one that works instantly! If he freaks out in that lift, we'll all be killed."

Dear, brave Pompeii did not freak out – he looked distinctly nervous as the floor sank beneath his feet, but I reassured him that it was not dangerous.

Back home, I looked in my wardrobe and was embarrassed. How could I possibly have so many clothes? After six months of managing perfectly well with two pairs of jeans and a T-shirt, and living among women who considered themselves lucky to have more than one pair of trousers, I was aghast. I had clothes hanging there that I had not worn for ten – twenty – years.

A shopping trip was even more traumatic.

The local supermarket was bloated with luxuries.

After spending six months in a country where fresh fruit was a rarity, I was staggered by the volume and variety of flowers, fruit and vegetables, much of it flown in from half a world away. How many airplanes, using how much fossil fuel, were in the air at this very moment, I wondered, so that spoilt people can have roses, artichokes or strawberries in December?

I drifted around the aisles, a stranger in my own back yard. Canned music swirled softly round my head. The smell of fresh bread was enticing. People were hurrying around me, pushing their silly, hard-to-steer carts as they completed their shopping as quickly as possible. Why were they in such a rush?

Fabric softener? Washing powder had been hard to come by, so the sight of half a dozen different varieties of fabric softener was shocking, or laughable. I couldn't decide which.

Breakfast cereals? The choice was so vast, I thought that if I actually wanted any cereal, it would take me all day to make up my mind which one to buy.

Whatever would Tatiana make of this cornucopia? Or Ura Kabil, one of the Cossacks I had set off with four months earlier. I remembered the conversation in which he had accused me of being a capitalist.

Obviously I was – or had been.

Would I become so again? Would I return to the old "me," over-worked, stressed out, buying "things" on a whim, worrying about un-important issues?

Or would I remain forever changed?

EPILOGUE

Pompeii and I safely back in England

"Why do we keep going round in circles?" Pompeii asked on one of our meaningless rides around the country. "Have you lost your compass? Every day we go out and then return to the same place where we started – crazy!"

"Silly boy! It's because we have arrived at the place we were travelling to!"

"Does that mean that for the rest of our lives we'll spend every night in the same place? How boring! I want to see new places, meet new people, shy at new horrors…. I want to LIVE, not just exist!"

"I know exactly how you feel, believe me. But we've had our adventure. Now we have to return to real life."

"If you say so," Pompeii grumbled unwillingly.

Pompeii was living at home, with my two old mares. His Cossack wives, however, had been turned out in an enormous paddock belonging to a friend. I checked them twice a day, but the mares had become very wild – so wild, in fact, that I had not been able to catch them to have their shoes removed.

After about a month they were fattening up nicely.

Especially the big black mare, whose belly was expanding rapidly.

"Oh my God, I do believe Masha's in foal," I thought to myself one cold day when I gave them their usual morning feed. I rang Mary and asked her to have a look and let me know what she thought.

"Yes, no doubt about it!" Mary reported back, laughing. "I reckon she's only got about two months to go."

So she must have conceived several weeks before we set off from Alexikovo.

Poor Masha! She had travelled 2,500 miles while pregnant – no wonder she had been a bit off-colour occasionally!

A week later I had a frantic telephone call from the owner of the field.

"You'd better come at once! Your white horse is down, and is all tangled up with the wire fence!"

I thanked him hurriedly, slammed the telephone down and called Andrew.

"Muffin's in trouble! It seems she's got in a muddle with the wire. Can you grab some wire-cutters, please?"

We jumped in the car and shot over to the paddock, a couple of miles away. Although I was concerned, I knew that Muffin could not have been lying in the mud for long, as I had checked the horses only an hour or so earlier.

Muffin was on her side, half under the hedge, which had been reinforced with wire. Masha was standing beside her friend, puzzled and worried. We approached the grey slowly, but she was quite calm. She knew I would help her. Close inspection revealed she had managed to get the wire jammed between her hoof and her shoe – on three of her feet!

"OK, you keep her calm and I'll cut the wire free," Andrew ordered. But it was not so easy. The sticky mud was everywhere, making Andrew's task nigh-on impossible. He struggled, he swore, he slipped.

"It's OK, Muffin. We'll get you out of there, don't worry," I said gently as I stroked her neck. She looked at me. How many times had I helped her when she had the tether-rope wrapped around her legs? She knew that if she just kept still, we humans would sort her out. I gently put a headcollar on her.

"She's free!" Andrew shouted in triumph. I stepped back and urged Muffin to get to her feet.

She was unhurt, and totally unconcerned.

"Can you try and grab Masha, please?" I asked Andrew. "If we can catch them both now, we can bung them in the stables."

For a non-horseman, Andrew did well. He took a very small handful of black mane and hung on. The big mare tried to pull away, found she could not do so without hurting herself, then stood resignedly while I put her headcollar on.

"I knew it couldn't last," she said to Muffin as we walked them back to the looseboxes. "We were so happy here, with plenty to eat and drink. Now I suppose they're going to take us to the slaughterhouse."

Instead of taking them to the slaughterhouse, we took them home, where they could easily be caught in my small paddocks.

The colt, a carbon copy of Pompeii, was born in March.

We called him Ashibka – mistake.

I had been looking for a job, as I urgently needed to start earning money again.

Two days after Ashibka's unexpected arrival, the telephone rang.

"Hello, this is Lloyd's Personnel department," said the woman on the other end. "We've got a temporary job available – can you start tomorrow?"

I was on the point of saying that I could not possibly work that week, but something made me say, "All right."

And so it was I fell into one of the best and most demanding jobs I ever had – Personal Assistant to one of the Directors of Lloyd's of London. It was to last until his retirement, four years later.

Luckily I found a good home for both mares and the foal: they went to a kind-hearted woman who promised to care for them for the rest of their lives.

But now I found it hard, very hard, to be one half of a couple.

"Why don't we leave?" Pompeii asked one evening while I hung up his night-time hay-net.

"Leave? Whatever do you mean?"

"You're so unhappy. You don't have to stay here, you know!"

"But Pompeii, that's an outrageous suggestion!"

"We horses can sense unhappiness, just as we can sense fear. Didn't you know that?"

"Well…. That makes sense, now you mention it. But I can't walk out on an 18-year marriage just like that! Andrew was incredibly supportive of our journey, you know."

Yet even as I spoke the words I realised that in reality I felt alienated. Resentful, even. Andrew was running around telling anyone who was prepared to listen that *his wife* had made this amazing trip, that he had found 126 messages from reporters on his answering machine, that *his wife* had been on television, in the newspapers, was famous……. Not once did I hear him say to anyone that I had done something special, something different, something slightly courageous.

"That's not enough!" Pompeii insisted.

"But I can't leave him – he loves me and needs me!"

"Humph!" he snorted. "You told me that Andrew built himself a lavish, panelled gun room (whatever that is), but never had enough money to extend the absurdly small kitchen you have to work in. I know how tiny it is – I've glimpsed it through the window."

"Yes, I know, but don't forget he paid quite a lot of money towards my trip. And you can't leave your husband just because he didn't give you a bigger kitchen!"

Pompeii was adamant. "You also told me that Andrew spent a fortune being flown in Russian fighter planes over Moscow last summer. And what about the twelve unusual cars parked all over the drive?"

"It's not about money, you know, Pompeii."

"No… except that you say you won't leave him because he loves you. Funny kind of love, always putting yourself first, that's what I say," and he blew down his nose contemptuously, and started tearing at his hay.

With a shock I realised that Pompeii was right. I had to escape.

And leave everything?

The house I loved so much, and into which I had invested so much love and energy?

Just a pile of bricks.

What about the furniture, china, silver, clothes and pictures I had so lovingly collected over thirty years? Just *things*.

The books? I could take the most precious ones with me.

I realised I was in gaol – imprisoned not by barbed wire and locks and gun-toting soldiers, but by my possessions, or, more accurately, by my love of those possessions.

Nine months after my return, I tacked Pompeii up one Sunday morning, swung into the saddle, and rode away.

Forever.

I had nowhere to live. Nowhere to go. It didn't matter.

Instead of feeling apprehensive about the future, I felt incredibly liberated. I had been trapped by my chattels, and in letting go of them I experienced a hitherto-unimagined freedom.

How much had I learned from Pompeii, how much he – and Russia – had taught me.

POST SCRIPT

Since my journey, I had been unable to talk to any of my old friends in any meaningful way. They did not understand what I had done, why I had done it, or how it had changed me.

For my part I could no longer understand them or their way of life with its emphasis on possessions and lack of any hint of challenge or danger.

Count Pompeii was safe in a good livery yard, and I was still working in London. Every weekend I went to the country and took him out for a ride.

I had no difficulty finding lodgings in London, and one evening in June 2000 I returned from work to find a letter on the mat.

It was from an American called CuChullaine O'Reilly. He had seen an article about my Russian journey in the British magazine *Horse and Hound*. He very politely said he would like to know more about the trip, and asked if I would like to join the Long Riders' Guild, an association he had formed for people who had made an equestrian journey of a thousand miles or more.

At the top of his letter I saw an email address.

Next morning I sent him a message. I had received his letter, I told him, and would be delighted to join the LRG.

CuChullaine himself had not only made the longest equestrian journey ever undertaken in Pakistan, but he had also spent decades studying equestrian travel.

He had written a book, *Khyber Knights*, which he had just completed.

So the emails started flying back and forth. We were so alike, it was almost frightening. After a month I picked up the telephone and rang him. For 45 minutes we talked and talked – we felt the same about everything.

It was not long after that that he asked me to marry him.

We knew each other far better, after our immense exchange of messages, than we would have done had we met at a cocktail party and dined together a few times. We knew absolutely everything about each other.

So of course I said "yes!"

CuChullaine told me that he was organising the first international meeting of Long Riders at his Kentucky home in early October, and therefore I took a fortnight off work so I could attend.

My family and friends reacted predictably.

"You can't just go to the USA to meet someone you've never seen! You don't know anything about him! You'll be found stabbed to death in a motel room!"

In other words, I was bombarded with the same negative fears as I had been before I went to Russia.

So I flew to the States and CuChullaine met me at the airport. We had never seen each other before, but that didn't matter.

I had found my soul-mate.

The following weekend we held the first meeting of Long Riders. It was quite extraordinary: we had all ridden in different parts of the world and met different problems, but our experiences were all the same. We literally didn't stop talking for three days.

I had found my tribe at last.

As soon as I could arrange everything I packed my few possessions and flew to Kentucky.

Pompeii went too, of course. He had to undergo a month's quarantine so I sent him on ahead. Without me to reassure him, he was very, very frightened until we met up together again shortly after he was released.

CuChullaine and I launched The Long Riders' Guild website in 2001 and since then the Guild has mentored, supported or equipped more than 150 equestrian expeditions in all parts of the world.

We started the Long Riders' Guild Press and brought back to life more than two hundred equestrian travel tales in five languages.

At the time of writing, we are in France.

I had understood by then that Pompeii didn't care where he was, as long as I took him there. So he and I flew back to Europe together in a cargo plane, but again the bureaucrats pounced.

"How much is he worth? Where are his papers?" "

I explained what a small amount I had paid for him and that he wasn't a recognised breed.

The officials arbitrarily said he was worth $5,000, and I faced a huge insurance bill as a result.

Nevertheless, we succeeded and had several happy years riding through the beautiful French countryside.

As an aside, Pompeii had better manners in terms of sex than some human males I have met and I never had the slightest problem when encountering mares. I put this down to his having been born "wild" on the Steppes and his mother and the other members of the herd teaching him how to behave.

CuChullaine completed the *Encyclopaedia of Equestrian Exploration*, a massive, three-volume work packed with history, anecdotes and advice from hundreds of Long Riders, living and dead. He also wrote the *Horse Travel*

Handbook, a book designed to fit in a saddle-bag and containing the essential information for a traveller to refer to while on the road.

In 2014 my beloved stallion died, peacefully. Not a moment has passed since, day or night, when he has not been in my thoughts and dreams.

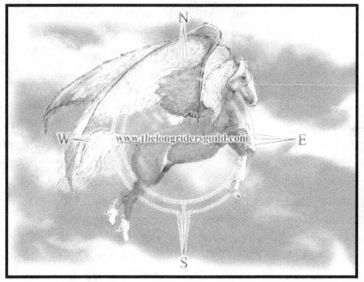

But he lives on – this image of him as a flying horse is the LRG logo, and is on the spine of every one of the hundreds of books we have published so far, including this one. It is also on the few LRG flags granted to people making exceptional journeys and has so far been carried in Africa, North America, South America, Australia, Siberia and Europe.

Basha O'Reilly
January 2017

Thelongridersguild.com   Classictravelbooks.com
Horsetravelbooks.com   Aimetschiffely.org
Lrgaf.org

Abdullah, Morag Mary, *My Khyber Marriage* - Morag Murray departed on a lifetime of adventure when she met and fell in love with Sirdar Ikbal Ali Shah, the son of an Afghan warlord. Leaving the comforts of her middle-class home in Scotland, Morag followed her husband into a Central Asia still largely unchanged since the 19th century.

Abernathy, Miles*, Ride the Wind* – the amazing true story of the little Abernathy Boys, who made a series of astonishing journeys in the United States, starting in 1909 when they were aged five and nine!

Atkinson, John, *Afghan Expedition* – The author travelled to Afghanistan in 1838. He had been designated the Superintending Surgeon of a massive British invasion force resolved to place a sympathetic ruler on the Afghan throne. Soon after Atkinson was released from duty, and thus escaped the catastrophe which awaited his comrades. The British political agent was beheaded and an estimated 16,000 British soldiers and their dependents were slaughtered in a week by the vengeful Afghans. This book is a must for anybody interested in Afghanistan – then and now.

Beard, John, *Saddles East* – John Beard determined as a child that he wanted to see the Wild West from the back of a horse after a visit to Cody's legendary Wild West show. Yet it was only in 1948 – more than sixty years after seeing the flamboyant American showman – that Beard and his wife Lulu finally set off to follow their dreams.

Beker, Ana, *The Courage to Ride* – Determined to out-do Tschiffely, Beker made a 17,000 mile mounted odyssey across the Americas in the late 1940s that would fix her place in the annals of equestrian travel history.

Bird, Isabella, *Among the Tibetans* – A rousing 1889 adventure, an enchanting travelogue, a forgotten peek at a mountain kingdom swept away by the waves of time.

Bird, Isabella, *On Horseback in Hawaii* – The Victorian explorer's first horseback journey, in which she learns to ride astride, in early 1873.

Bird, Isabella, *Journeys in Persia and Kurdistan, Volumes 1 and 2* – The intrepid Englishwoman undertakes another gruelling journey in 1890.

Bird, Isabella, *A Lady's Life in the Rocky Mountains* – The story of Isabella Bird's adventures during the winter of 1873 when she explored the magnificent unspoiled wilderness of Colorado. Truly a classic.

Bird, Isabella, *Unbeaten Tracks in Japan, Volumes One and Two* – A 600-mile solo ride through Japan undertaken by the intrepid British traveller in 1878.

Blackmore, Charles, *In the Footsteps of Lawrence of Arabia* - In February 1985 Captain Charles Blackmore and three others of the Royal Green Jackets Regiment set out to retrace Lawrence's exploits in the Arab Revolt during the First World War.

Boniface, Lieutenant Jonathan, *The Cavalry Horse and his Pack* – Quite simply the most important book ever written in the English language by a military man on the subject of equestrian travel.

Bosanquet, Mary, *Saddlebags for Suitcases* – In 1939 Bosanquet set out to ride from Vancouver, Canada, to New York. Along the way she was wooed by love-struck cowboys, chased by a grizzly bear and even suspected of being a Nazi spy, scouting out Canada in preparation for a German invasion. A truly delightful book.

de Bourboulon, Catherine, *Shanghai à Moscou (French)* – the story of how a young Scottish woman and her aristocratic French husband travelled overland from Shanghai to Moscow in the late 19th Century.

Brown, Donald; *Journey from the Arctic* – A truly remarkable account of how Brown, his Danish companion and their two trusty horses attempt the impossible, to cross the silent Arctic plateaus, thread their way through the giant Swedish forests, and finally discover a passage around the treacherous Norwegian marshes.

Bruce, Clarence Dalrymple, *In the Hoofprints of Marco Polo* – The author made a dangerous journey from Srinagar to Peking in 1905, mounted on a trusty 13-hand Kashmiri pony, then wrote this wonderful book.

Burnaby, Frederick; *A Ride to Khiva* – Burnaby fills every page with a memorable cast of characters, including hard-riding Cossacks, nomadic Tartars, vodka-guzzling sleigh-drivers and a legion of peasant ruffians.

Burnaby, Frederick, *On Horseback through Asia Minor* – Armed with a rifle, a small stock of medicines, and a single faithful servant, the equestrian traveler rode through a hotbed of intrigue and high adventure in wild inhospitable country, encountering Kurds, Circassians, Armenians, and Persian pashas.

Carter, General William, *Horses, Saddles and Bridles* – This book covers a wide range of topics including basic training of the horse and care of its equipment. It also provides a fascinating look back into equestrian travel history.

Cayley, George, *Bridle Roads of Spain* – Truly one of the greatest equestrian travel accounts of the 19th Century.

Chase, J. Smeaton, *California Coast Trails* – This classic book describes the author's journey from Mexico to Oregon along the coast of California in the 1890s.

Chase, J. Smeaton, *California Desert Trails* – Famous British naturalist J. Smeaton Chase mounted up and rode into the Mojave Desert to undertake the longest equestrian study of its kind in modern history.

Chitty, Susan, and Hinde, Thomas, *The Great Donkey Walk* - When biographer Susan Chitty and her novelist husband, Thomas Hinde, decided it was time to embark on a family adventure, they did it in style. In Santiago they bought two donkeys whom they named Hannibal and Hamilcar. Their two small daughters, Miranda (7) and Jessica (3) were to ride Hamilcar. Hannibal, meanwhile, carried the baggage. The walk they planned to undertake was nothing short of the breadth of southern Europe.

Christian, Glynn, *Fragile Paradise: The discovery of Fletcher Christian, "Bounty" Mutineer* – the great-great-great-great-grandson of the *Bounty* mutineer brings to life a fascinating and complex character history has portrayed as both hero and villain, and the real story behind a mutiny that continues to divide opinion more than 200 years later.

Christian, Glynn, *Mrs Christian: Bounty Mutineer* - This is the heroic and bloody untold story of Mauatua, Tahitian lover and wife of BOUNTY mutineer Fletcher Christian and of what she and 11 other women endured to survive on Pitcairn Island, the mutineers' secret refuge for almost twenty years.

Clark, Leonard, *Marching Wind, The* – The panoramic story of a mounted exploration in the remote and savage heart of Asia, a place where adventure, danger, and intrigue were the daily backdrop to wild tribesman and equestrian exploits.

Clark, Leonard, *A Wanderer Till I Die* – In a world with lax passport control, no airlines, and few rules, this young man floats effortlessly from one adventure to the next. When he's not drinking whisky at the Raffles Hotel or listening to the "St. Louis Blues" on the phonograph in the jungle, he's searching for Malaysian treasure, being captured by Toradja head-hunters, interrogated by Japanese intelligence officers and lured into shady deals by European gun-runners.

Cobbett, William, *Rural Rides, Volumes 1 and 2* – In the early 1820s Cobbett set out on horseback to make a series of personal tours through the English countryside. These books contain what many believe to be the best accounts of rural England ever written, and remain enduring classics.

Codman, John, *Winter Sketches from the Saddle* – This classic book was first published in 1888. It recommends riding for your health and describes the septuagenarian author's many equestrian journeys through New England during the winter of 1887 on his faithful mare, Fanny.

Cunninghame Graham, Jean, *Gaucho Laird* – A superbly readable biography of the author's famous great-uncle, Robert "Don Roberto" Cunninghame Graham.

Cunninghame Graham, Robert, *Horses of the Conquest* – The author uncovered manuscripts which had lain forgotten for centuries, and wrote this book, as he said, out of gratitude to the horses of Columbus and the Conquistadors who shaped history.

Cunninghame Graham, Robert, *Magreb-el-Acksa* – The thrilling tale of how "Don Roberto" was kidnapped in Morocco!

Cunninghame Graham, Robert, *Rodeo* – An omnibus of the finest work of the man they called "the uncrowned King of Scotland," edited by his friend Aimé Tschiffely.

Cunninghame Graham, Robert, *Tales of Horsemen* – Ten of the most beautifully-written equestrian stories ever set to paper.

Cunninghame Graham, Robert, *Vanished Arcadia* – This haunting story about the Jesuit missions in South America from 1550 to 1767 was the inspiration behind the best-selling film *The Mission*.

Daly, H.W., *Manual of Pack Transportation* – This book is the author's masterpiece. It contains a wealth of information on various pack saddles, ropes and equipment, how to secure every type of load imaginable and instructions on how to organize a pack train.

Dixie, Lady Florence, *Riding Across Patagonia* – When asked in 1879 why she wanted to travel to such an outlandish place as Patagonia, the author replied without hesitation that she was taking to the saddle in order to flee from the strict confines of polite Victorian society. This is the story of how the aristocrat successfully traded the perils of a London parlour for the wind-borne freedom of a wild Patagonian bronco.

Dodwell, Christina, *Beyond Siberia* – The intrepid author goes to Russia's Far East to join the reindeer-herding people in winter.

Dodwell, Christina, *An Explorer's Handbook* – The author tells you everything you want to know about travelling: how to find suitable pack animals, how to feed and shelter yourself. She also has sensible and entertaining advice about dealing with unwanted visitors and the inevitable bureaucrats.

Dodwell, Christina, *Madagascar Travels* – Christina explores the hidden corners of this amazing island and, as usual, makes friends with its people.

Dodwell, Christina, *A Traveller in China* – The author sets off alone across China, starting with a horse and then transferring to an inflatable canoe.

Dodwell, Christina, *A Traveller on Horseback* – Christina Dodwell rides through Eastern Turkey and Iran in the late 1980s. The Sunday Telegraph wrote of the author's "courage and insatiable wanderlust," and in this book she demonstrates her gift for communicating her zest for adventure.

Dodwell, Christina, *Travels in Papua New Guinea* – Christina Dodwell spends two years exploring an island little known to the outside world. She travelled by foot, horse and dugout canoe among the Stone-Age tribes.

Dodwell, Christina, *Travels with Fortune* – the truly amazing account of the courageous author's first journey – a three-year odyssey around Africa by Landrover, bus, lorry, horse, camel, and dugout canoe!

Dodwell, Christina, *Travels with Pegasus* – This time Christina takes to the air! This is the story of her unconventional journey across North Africa in a micro-light!

Downey, Bill - *Whisper on the Wind - The Story of Tom Bass, Celebrated Black Horseman* - Tom Bass rose to the summit of what had always been a white man's profession, the training of the America's greatest Saddlebred horses. An advocate of gentleness and patience, Bass turned dangerous horses into reliable mounts - without ever raising his voice or using a whip.

Duncan, John, *Travels in Western Africa in 1845 and 1846* – The author, a Lifeguardsman from Scotland, tells the hair-raising tale of his two journeys to what is now Benin. Sadly, Duncan has been forgotten until today, and we are proud to get this book back into print.

Ehlers, Otto, *Im Sattel durch die Fürstenhöfe Indiens* – In June 1890 the young German adventurer, Ehlers, lay very ill. His doctor gave him a choice: either go home to Germany or travel to Kashmir. So of course the Long Rider chose the latter. This is a thrilling yet humorous book about the author's adventures.

Farson, Negley, *Caucasian Journey* – A thrilling account of a dangerous equestrian journey made in 1929, this is an amply illustrated adventure classic.

Fox, Ernest, *Travels in Afghanistan* – The thrilling tale of a 1937 journey through the mountains, valleys, and deserts of this forbidden realm, including visits to such fabled places as the medieval city of Heart, the towering Hindu Kush mountains, and the legendary Khyber Pass.

Gall, Sandy, *Afghanistan – Agony of a Nation* - Sandy Gall has made three trips to Afghanistan to report the war there: in 1982, 1984 and again in 1986. This book is an account of his last journey and what he found.

Gall, Sandy, *Behind Russian Lines* – In the summer of 1982, Sandy Gall set off for Afghanistan on what turned out to be the hardest assignment of his life. During his career as a reporter he had covered plenty of wars and revolutions before, but this was the first time he had been required to walk all the way to an assignment and all the way back again, dodging Russian bombs *en route*.

Galton, Francis, *The Art of Travel* – Originally published in 1855, this book became an instant classic and was used by a host of now-famous explorers, including Sir Richard Francis Burton of Mecca fame. Readers can learn how to ride horses, handle elephants, avoid cobras, pull teeth, find water in a desert, and construct a sleeping bag out of fur.

Glazier, Willard, *Ocean to Ocean on Horseback* – This book about the author's journey from New York to the Pacific in 1875 contains every kind of mounted adventure imaginable. Amply illustrated with pen and ink drawings of the time, this remains a timeless equestrian adventure classic.

Goodwin, Joseph, *Through Mexico on Horseback* – The author and his companion, Robert Horiguichi, the sophisticated, multi-lingual son of an imperial Japanese diplomat, set out in 1931 to cross Mexico. They were totally unprepared for the deserts, quicksand and brigands they were to encounter during their adventure.

Gordon, W. J., *The Horse World of Victorian London* – An enthralling and unforgettable study of the work undertaken by horses before the invention of the car.

Grant, David, *Spirit of the Vikings: A Journey in the Kayak Bahá'í Viking From Arkosund, Sweden, to Odessa, Ukraine* – David Grant takes his kayak on an adventure-filled and spiritual journey from Sweden to Odessa on the Black Sea.

Grant, David, *The Wagon Travel Handbook* - David Grant is the legendary Scottish wagon-master who journeyed around the world with his family in a horse-drawn wagon. Grant has filled *The Wagon Travel Handbook* with all the practical information a first time-wagon traveller will need before setting out.

Gray, David and Lukas Novotny, *Mounted Archery in the Americas* – This fascinating and amply illustrated book charts the history of mounted archery from its ancient roots on the steppes of Eurasia thousands of years ago to its current resurgence in popularity in the Americas. It also provides the reader with up-to-the-minute practical information gleaned from a unique team of the world's leading experts.

Hamilton Smith, Charles, *Equus: The Natural History of the Horse, Ass, Onager, Quagga and Zebra* - A masterpiece of erudition. The author was concerned that the public was being misled by erroneous accounts or the absence of accurate information. To rectify this error, he set about enabling equestrian essentials to emerge from obscurity, thereby authoring a book which became the principal authority on all aspects of horse-related wisdom.

Hanbury-Tenison, Marika, *For Better, For Worse* – The author, an excellent story-teller, writes about her adventures visiting and living among the Indians of Central Brazil.

Hanbury-Tenison, Marika, *A Slice of Spice* – The fresh and vivid account of the author's hazardous journey to the Indonesian Islands with her husband, Robin.

Hanbury-Tenison, Robin, *Chinese Adventure* – The story of a unique journey in which the explorer Robin Hanbury-Tenison and his wife Louella rode on horseback alongside the Great Wall of China in 1986.

Hanbury-Tenison, Robin, *Fragile Eden* – The wonderful story of Robin and Louella Hanbury-Tenison's exploration of New Zealand on horseback in 1988. They rode alone together through what they describe as 'some of the most dramatic and exciting country we have ever seen.'

Hanbury-Tenison, Robin, *Mulu: The Rainforest* – This was the first popular book to bring to the world's attention the significance of the rain forests to our fragile ecosystem. It is a timely reminder of our need to preserve them for the future.

Hanbury-Tenison, Robin, *A Pattern of Peoples* – The author and his wife, Marika, spent three months travelling through Indonesia's outer islands and writes with his usual flair and sensitivity about the tribes he found there.

Hanbury-Tenison, Robin, *A Question of Survival* – This superb book played a hugely significant role in bringing the plight of Brazil's Indians to the world's attention.

Hanbury-Tenison, Robin, *The Rough and the Smooth* – The incredible story of two journeys in South America. Neither had been attempted before, and both were considered impossible!

Hanbury-Tenison, Robin, *Spanish Pilgrimage* – Robin and Louella Hanbury-Tenison went to Santiago de Compostela in a traditional way – riding on white horses over long-forgotten tracks. In the process they discovered more about the people and the country than any conventional traveller would learn. Their adventures are vividly and entertainingly recounted in this delightful and highly readable book.

Hanbury-Tenison, Robin, *White Horses over France* – This enchanting book tells the story of a magical journey and how, in fulfilment of a personal dream, the first Camargue horses set foot on British soil in the late summer of 1984.

Hanbury-Tenison, Robin, *Worlds Apart – an Explorer's Life* – The author's battle to preserve the quality of life under threat from developers and machines infuses this autobiography with a passion and conviction which makes it impossible to put down.

Hanbury-Tenison, Robin, *Worlds Within – Reflections in the Sand* – This book is full of the adventure you would expect from a man of action like Robin Hanbury-Tenison. However, it is also filled with the type of rare knowledge that was revealed to other desert travellers like Lawrence, Doughty and Thesiger.

Haslund, Henning, *Mongolian Adventure* – An epic tale inhabited by a cast of characters no longer present in this lackluster world, shamans who set themselves on fire, rebel leaders who sacked towns, and wild horsemen whose ancestors conquered the world.

Hassanein, A. M., *The Lost Oases* - At the dawning of the 20th century the vast desert of Libya remained one of last unexplored places on Earth. Sir Hassanein Bey befriended the Muslim leaders of the elusive Senussi Brotherhood who controlled the deserts further on, and became aware of rumours of a "lost oasis" which lay even deeper in the desert. In 1923 the explorer led a small caravan on a remarkable seven month journey across the centre of Libya.

Heath, Frank, *Forty Million Hoofbeats* – Heath set out in 1925 to follow his dream of riding to all 48 of the Continental United States. The journey lasted more than two years, during which time Heath and his mare, Gypsy Queen, became inseparable companions.

Hinde, Thomas, *The Great Donkey Walk* – Biographer Susan Chitty and her novelist husband, Thomas Hinde, travelled from Spain's Santiago to Salonica in faraway Greece. Their two small daughters, Miranda (7) and Jessica (3) were rode one donkey, while the other donkey carried the baggage. Reading this delightful book is leisurely and continuing pleasure.

Holt, William, *Ride a White Horse* – After rescuing a cart horse, Trigger, from slaughter and nursing him back to health, the 67-year-old Holt and his horse set out in 1964 on an incredible 9,000 mile, non-stop journey through western Europe.

Hope, Thomas, *Anastasius* – Here is the book that took the world by storm, and then was forgotten. Hope's hero Anastasius was fearless, curious, cunning, ruthless, brave, and above all, sexy. He journeyed deep into the vast and dangerous Ottoman Empire. During the 35 years described in the book (1762-1798) the swashbuckling hero infiltrated the deadly Wahhabis in Arabia, rode to war with the Mamelukes in Egypt and sailed the Mediterranean with the Turks. This remarkable new edition features all three volumes together for the first time.

Hopkins, Frank T., *Hidalgo and Other Stories* – For the first time in history, here are the collected writings of Frank T. Hopkins, the counterfeit cowboy whose endurance racing claims and Old West fantasies have polarized the equestrian world.

Jebb, Louisa, *By Desert Ways to Baghdad and Damascus* – From the pen of a gifted writer and intrepid traveller, this is one of the greatest equestrian travel books of all time.

Kluckhohn, Clyde, *To the Foot of the Rainbow* – This is not just a exciting true tale of equestrian adventure. It is a moving account of a young man's search for physical perfection in a desert world still untouched by the recently-born twentieth century.

Lambie, Thomas, *Boots and Saddles in Africa* – Lambie's story of his equestrian journeys is told with the grit and realism that marks a true classic.

Landor, Henry Savage, *In the Forbidden Land* – Illustrated with hundreds of photographs and drawings, this blood-chilling account of equestrian adventure makes for page-turning excitement.

Langlet, Valdemar, *Till Häst Genom Ryssland (Swedish)* – Denna reseskildring rymmer många ögonblicksbilder av möten med människor, från morgonbad med Lev Tolstoi till samtal med Tartarer och fotografering av fagra skördeflickor. Rikt illustrerad med foto och teckningar.

Leigh, Margaret, *My Kingdom for a Horse* – In the autumn of 1939 the author rode from Cornwall to Scotland, resulting in one of the most delightful equestrian journeys of the early twentieth century. This book is full of keen observations of a rural England that no longer exists.

Lester, Mary, *A Lady's Ride across Spanish Honduras in 1881* – This is a gem of a book, with a very entertaining account of Mary's vivid, day-to-day life in the saddle.

MacDermot, Brian, *Cult of the Sacred Spear* – here is that rarest of travel books, an exploration not only of a distant land but of a man's own heart. A confederation of pastoral people located in Southern Sudan and western Ethiopia, the Nuer warriors were famous for staging cattle raids against larger tribes and successfully resisted European colonization. Brian MacDermot, London stockbroker, entered into Nuer society as a stranger and

Maeterlinck, Maurice, *Clever Hans and the Elberfeld Horses* – In the early 20th Century, a German stallion named Clever Hans could apparently communicate with humans. The discovery of this remarkable animal, who could supposedly also spell and tell time, caused such an uproar that the German government appointed the "Hans Commission" to investigate the astonishing claims.

Maillart, Ella, *Turkestan Solo* – A vivid account of a 1930s journey through this wonderful, mysterious and dangerous portion of the world, with its Kirghiz eagle hunters, lurking Soviet secret police, and the timeless nomads that still inhabited the desolate steppes of Central Asia.

Marcy, Randolph, *The Prairie Traveler* – There were a lot of things you packed into your saddlebags or the wagon before setting off to cross the North American wilderness in the 1850s. A gun and an axe were obvious necessities. Yet many pioneers were just as adamant about placing a copy of Captain Randolph Marcy's classic book close at hand.

Marsden, Kate, *Riding through Siberia: A Mounted Medical Mission in 1891* – This immensely readable book is a mixture of adventure, extreme hardship and compassion as the author travels the Great Siberian Post Road.

Marsh, Hippisley Cunliffe, *A Ride Through Islam* – A British officer rides through Persia and Afghanistan to India in 1873. Full of adventures, and with observant remarks on the local Turkoman equestrian traditions.

MacCann, William, *Viaje a Caballo* – Spanish-language edition of the British author's equestrian journey around Argentina in 1848.

Mason, Theodore, *The South Pole Ponies* – The touching and totally forgotten story of the little horses who gave their all to both Scott and Shackleton in their attempts to reach the South Pole.

Meline, James, *Two Thousand Miles on Horseback: Kansas to Santa Fé in 1866* – A beautifully written, eye witness account of a United States that is no more.

Muir Watson, Sharon, *The Colour of Courage* – The remarkable true story of the epic horse trip made by the first people to travel Australia's then-unmarked Bicentennial National Trail. There are enough adventures here to satisfy even the most jaded reader.

Naysmith, Gordon, *The Will to Win* – This book recounts the only equestrian journey of its kind undertaken during the 20th century - a mounted trip stretching across 16 countries. Gordon Naysmith, a Scottish pentathlete and former military man, set out in 1970 to ride from the tip of the African continent to the 1972 Olympic Games in distant Germany.

Ondaatje, Christopher, *Leopard in the Afternoon* – The captivating story of a journey through some of Africa's most spectacular haunts. It is also touched with poignancy and regret for a vanishing wilderness – a world threatened with extinction.

Ondaatje, Christopher, *The Man-Eater of Pununai* – a fascinating story of a past rediscovered through a remarkable journey to one of the most exotic countries in the world — Sri Lanka. Full of drama and history, it not only relives the incredible story of a man-eating leopard that terrorized the tiny village of Punanai in the early part of the century, but also allows the author to come to terms with the ghost of his charismatic but tyrannical father.

www.horsetravelbooks.com

Ondaatje, Christopher, *Sindh Revisited* – This is the extraordinarily sensitive account of the author's quest to uncover the secrets of the seven years Richard Burton spent in India in the army of the East India Company from 1842 to 1849. **O'Connor, Derek,** *The King's Stranger* – a superb biography of the forgotten Scottish explorer, John Duncan.

O'Reilly, Basha, *Bandits and Bureaucrats* – the story of a journey from Russia to England.

O'Reilly, Basha, *Count Pompeii – Stallion of the Steppes* – the story of Basha's journey from Russia with her stallion, Count Pompeii, told for children. This is the first book in the *Little Long Rider* series.

O'Reilly, CuChullaine, *Deadly Equines: the Shocking True Story of Meat-Eating and Murderous Horses.* What if a Rosetta Stone had been found to unlock the dark secrets of the horse's past? What if evidence demonstrated horses have slain lions, tigers, pumas, wolves, hyenas and humans? What if testimony revealed meat-eating horses had been used to explore the Poles and photographs had been discovered of Tibet's blood-eating horses? *Deadly Equines* is a revolutionary departure from equestrian romance. It is a fact-filled analysis which reveals how humanity has known about meat-eating horses for at least four thousand years, and that these episodes have occurred on every continent, including Antarctica.

O'Reilly, CuChullaine, *The Encyclopaedia of Equestrian Exploration* - a massive, three-volume work packed with history, anecdotes and advice from hundreds of Long Riders, living and dead.

O'Reilly, CuChullaine, (Editor) *The Horse Travel Handbook* – this accumulated knowledge of a million miles in the saddle tells you everything you need to know about travelling with your horse!

O'Reilly, CuChullaine, (Editor) *The Horse Travel Journal* – a unique book to take on your ride and record your experiences. Includes the world's first equestrian travel "pictionary" to help you in foreign countries.

O'Reilly, CuChullaine, *Khyber Knights* – Told with grit and realism by one of the world's foremost equestrian explorers, "Khyber Knights" has been penned the way lives are lived, not how books are written.

O'Reilly, CuChullaine, (Editor) *The Long Riders, Volume One* – The first of five unforgettable volumes of exhilarating travel tales.

Östrup, J, *(Swedish), Växlande Horisont* – The thrilling account of the author's journey to Central Asia from 1891 to 1893.

Patterson, George, *Gods and Guerrillas* – The true and gripping story of how the author went secretly into Tibet to film the Chinese invaders of his adopted country. Will make your heart pound with excitement!

Patterson, George, *Journey with Loshay: A Tibetan Odyssey* – This is an amazing book written by a truly remarkable man! Relying both on his companionship with God and on his own strength, he undertook a life few can have known, and a journey of emergency across the wildest parts of Tibet.

Patterson, George, *Patterson of Tibet* –This intense autobiography reveals how Patterson crossed swords with India's Prime Minister Nehru, helped with the rescue of the Dalai Lama and befriended a host of unique world figures ranging from Yehudi Menhuin to Eric Clapton. This is a vividly-written account of a life of high adventure and spiritual odyssey.

Pocock, Roger, *Following the Frontier* – Pocock was one of the nineteenth century's most influential equestrian travelers. Within the covers of this book is the detailed account of Pocock's horse ride along the infamous Outlaw Trail, a 3,000 mile solo journey that took the adventurer from Canada to Mexico City.

Pocock, Roger, *Horses* – Pocock set out to document the wisdom of the late 19th and early 20th Centuries into a book unique for its time. His concerns for attempting to preserve equestrian knowledge were based on cruel reality. More than 300,000 horses had been destroyed during the recent Boer War. Though Pocock enjoyed a reputation for dangerous living, his observations on horses were praised by the leading thinkers of his day.

Post, Charles Johnson, *Horse Packing* – Originally published in 1914, this book was an instant success, incorporating as it did the very essence of the science of packing horses and mules. It makes fascinating reading for students of the horse or history.

Ray, G. W., *Through Five Republics on Horseback* – In 1889 a British explorer – part-time missionary and full-time adventure junky – set out to find a lost tribe of sun-worshipping natives in the unexplored forests of Paraguay. The journey was so brutal that it defies belief.

Rink, Bjarke, *The Centaur Legacy* – This immensely entertaining and historically important book provides the first ever in-depth study into how man's partnership with his equine companion changed the course of history and accelerated human development.

Ross, Martin and Somerville, E, *Beggars on Horseback* – The hilarious adventures of two aristocratic Irish cousins on an 1894 riding tour of Wales.

Ruxton, George, *Adventures in Mexico* – The story of a young British army officer who rode from Vera Cruz to Santa Fe, Mexico in 1847. At times the author exhibits a fearlessness which borders on insanity. He ignores dire warnings, rides through deadly deserts, and dares murderers to attack him. It is a delightful and invigorating tale of a time and place now long gone.

von Salzman, Erich, *Im Sattel durch Zentralasien* – The astonishing tale of the author's journey through China, Turkistan and back to his home in Germany – 6000 kilometres in 176 days!

Schwarz, Hans *(German)*, *Vier Pferde, Ein Hund und Drei Soldaten* – In the early 1930s the author and his two companions rode through Liechtenstein, Austria, Romania, Albania, Yugoslavia, to Turkey, then rode back again!

Schwarz, Otto *(German)*, *Reisen mit dem Pferd* – the Swiss Long Rider with more miles in the saddle than anyone else tells his wonderful story, and a long appendix tells the reader how to follow in his footsteps.

Scott, Robert, *Scott's Last Expedition* – Many people are unaware that Scott recruited Yakut ponies from Siberia for his doomed expedition to the South Pole in 1909. Here is the remarkable story of men and horses who all paid the ultimate sacrifice.

Shackleton, Ernest, *Aurora Australis* - The members of the British Antarctic Expedition of 1907-1908 wrote this delightful and surprisingly funny book. It was printed on the spot "at the sign of the Penguin"!

Skrede, Wilfred, *Across the Roof of the World* – This epic equestrian travel tale of a wartime journey across Russia, China, Turkestan and India is laced with unforgettable excitement.

Stevens, Thomas, *Through Russia on a Mustang* – Mounted on his faithful horse, Texas, Stevens crossed the Steppes in search of adventure. Cantering across the pages of this classic tale is a cast of nineteenth century Russian misfits, peasants, aristocrats—and even famed Cossack Long Rider Dmitri Peshkov.

Stevenson, Robert L., *Travels with a Donkey* – In 1878, the author set out to explore the remote Cevennes mountains of France. He travelled alone, unless you count his stubborn and manipulative pack-donkey, Modestine. This book is a true classic.

Strong, Anna Louise, *Road to the Grey Pamir* – With Stalin's encouragement, Strong rode into the seldom-seen Pamir mountains of faraway Tadjikistan. The political renegade turned equestrian explorer soon discovered more adventure than she had anticipated.

Sykes, Ella, *Through Persia on a Sidesaddle* – Ella Sykes rode side-saddle 2,000 miles across Persia, a country few European woman had ever visited. Mind you, she traveled in style, accompanied by her Swiss maid and 50 camels loaded with china, crystal, linens and fine wine.

Trinkler, Emile, *Through the Heart of Afghanistan* – In the early 1920s the author made a legendary trip across a country now recalled only in legends.

Tschiffely, Aimé, *Bohemia Junction* – "Forty years of adventurous living condensed into one book."

Tschiffely, Aimé, *Bridle Paths* – a final poetic look at a now-vanished Britain.

Tschiffely, Aimé, *Coricancha*: A fascinating and balanced account of the conquest of the Inca Empire.

Tschiffely, Aimé, *Don Roberto* – A biography of Tschiffely's friend and mentor, Robert Cunninghame Graham.

Tschiffely, Aimé, *Little Princess Turtle Dove* – An enchanting fairy story set in South America and displaying Aimé Tschiffely's love, not only for children and animals, but also for South America.

Tschiffely, Aimé, *Mancha y Gato Cuentan sus Aventuras* – The Spanish-language version of *The Tale of Two Horses* – the story of the author's famous journey as told by the horses.

Tschiffely, Aimé, *Ming and Ping*: An adventure book for older children. The title characters go exploring South America together. They meet many tribes of Indians and learn about their way of life. Exhilarating and effortlessly instructive.

Tschiffely, Aimé, *Round and About Spain:* Tschiffely sets off to explore Spain, but this time his steed is a motorbike, not a horse! With wit, wisdom and a sharp eye for the absurd, he travels to all four corners of this fascinating country and makes many friends along the way. So much has changed since the Second World War that that this book is a unique snapshot of Spain as she was in 1950.

Tschiffely, Aimé, *The Tale of Two Horses* – The story of Tschiffely's famous journey from Buenos Aires to Washington, DC, narrated by his two equine heroes, Mancha and Gato. Their unique point of view is guaranteed to delight children and adults alike.

Tschiffely, Aimé, *This Way Southward* – the most famous equestrian explorer of the twentieth century decides to make a perilous journey across the U-boat infested Atlantic.

Tschiffely, Aimé, *Tschiffely's Ride* – The true story of the most famous equestrian journey of the twentieth century – 10,000 miles with two Criollo geldings from Argentina to Washington, DC. A new edition is coming soon with a Foreword by his literary heir!

Tschiffely, Aimé, *Tschiffely's Ritt* – The German-language translation of *Tschiffely's Ride* – the most famous equestrian journey of its day.

Ure, John, *Cucumber Sandwiches in the Andes* – No-one who wasn't mad as a hatter would try to take a horse across the Andes by one of the highest passes between Chile and the Argentine. That was what John Ure was told on his way to the British Embassy in Santiago – so he set out to find a few certifiable kindred spirits. Fans of equestrian travel and of Latin America will be enchanted by this delightful book.

Warner, Charles Dudley, *On Horseback in Virginia* – A prolific author, and a great friend of Mark Twain, Warner made witty and perceptive contributions to the world of nineteenth century American literature. This book about the author's equestrian adventures is full of fascinating descriptions of nineteenth century America.

Weale, Magdalene, *Through the Highlands of Shropshire* – It was 1933 and Magdalene Weale was faced with a dilemma: how to best explore her beloved English countryside? By horse, of course! This enchanting book invokes a gentle, softer world inhabited by gracious country lairds, wise farmers, and jolly inn keepers.

Weeks, Edwin Lord, *Artist Explorer* – A young American artist and superb writer travels through Persia to India in 1892.

Wentworth Day, J., *Wartime Ride* – In 1939 the author decided the time was right for an extended horseback ride through England! While parts of his country were being ravaged by war, Wentworth Day discovered an inland oasis of mellow harvest fields, moated Tudor farmhouses, peaceful country halls, and fishing villages.

Von Westarp, Eberhard, *Unter Halbmond und Sonne* – (German) – Im Sattel durch die asiatische Türkei und Persien.

Wilkins, Messanie, *Last of the Saddle Tramps* – Told she had little time left to live, the author decided to ride from her native Maine to the Pacific. Accompanied by her faithful horse, Tarzan, Wilkins suffered through any number of obstacles, including blistering deserts and freezing snow storms – and defied the doctors by living for another 20 years!

Wilson, Andrew, *The Abode of Snow* – One of the best accounts of overland equestrian travel ever written about the wild lands that lie between Tibet and Afghanistan.

de Windt, Harry, *A Ride to India* – Part science, all adventure, this book takes the reader for a thrilling canter across the Persian Empire of the 1890s.

Winthrop, Theodore, *Saddle and Canoe* – This book paints a vibrant picture of 1850s life in the Pacific Northwest and covers the author's travels along the Straits of Juan De Fuca, on Vancouver Island, across the Naches Pass, and on to The Dalles, in Oregon Territory. This is truly an historic travel account.

Woolf, Leonard, *Stories of the East* – Three short stories which are of vital importance in understanding the author's mistrust of and dislike for colonialism, which provide disturbing commentaries about the disintegration of the colonial process.

Younghusband, George, *Eighteen Hundred Miles on a Burmese Pony* – One of the funniest and most enchanting books about equestrian travel of the nineteenth century, featuring "Joe" the naughty Burmese pony!

CPSIA information can be obtained
at www.ICGtesting.com
Printed in the USA
LVHW091610070521
686791LV00006B/870